PRACTICE – ASSESS – DIAGNO

180 Days of PROBLEM SOLVING
for Second Grade

- ? Think
- Plan
- Solve
- Explain

232 > 145

Author
Donna Ventura, M.A.Ed.

SHELL EDUCATION

For information on how this resource meets national and other state standards, see page 4. You may also review this information by visiting our website at www.teachercreatedmaterials.com/administrators/correlations/ and following the on-screen directions.

Publishing Credits

Corinne Burton, M.A.Ed., *Publisher*; Conni Medina, M.A.Ed., *Managing Editor*; Emily R. Smith, M.A.Ed., *Series Developer*; Diana Kenney, M.A.Ed., NBCT, *Content Director*; Paula Makridis, M.A.Ed., *Editor*; Lee Aucoin, *Senior Multimedia Designer*; Kyleena Harper, *Assistant Editor*; Kevin Pham, *Graphic Designer*

Image Credits

All images from iStock and Shutterstock.

Standards

Shell Education

A division of Teacher Created Materials
5301 Oceanus Drive
Huntington Beach, CA 92649-1030

www.tcmpub.com/shell-education
ISBN 978-1-4258-1614-8
©2017 Shell Education Publishing, Inc.

TABLE OF CONTENTS

INTRODUCTION

The Need for Practice

To be successful in today's mathematics classrooms, students must deeply understand both concepts and procedures so that they can discuss and demonstrate their understanding during the problem-solving process. Demonstrating understanding is a process that must be continually practiced for students to be successful. Practice is especially important to help students apply their concrete, conceptual understanding during each step of the problem-solving process.

Understanding Assessment

In addition to providing opportunities for frequent practice, teachers must be able to assess students' problem-solving skills. This is important so that teachers can adequately address students' misconceptions, build on their current understandings, and challenge them appropriately. Assessment is a long-term process that involves careful analysis of student responses from discussions, projects, practice pages, or tests. When analyzing the data, it is important for teachers to reflect on how their teaching practices may have influenced students' responses and to identify those areas where additional instruction may be required. In short, the data gathered from assessments should be used to inform instruction: slow down, speed up, or reteach. This type of assessment is called *formative assessment*.

HOW TO USE THIS BOOK

180 Days of Problem Solving offers teachers and parents problem-solving activities for each day of the school year. Students will build their problem-solving skills as they develop a deeper understanding of mathematical concepts and apply these concepts to real-life situations. This series will also help students improve their critical-thinking and reasoning skills, use visual models when solving problems, approach problems in multiple ways, and solve multi-step, non-routine word problems.

Easy-to-Use and Standards-Based

These daily activities reinforce grade-level skills across a variety of mathematical concepts. Each day provides a full practice page, making the activities easy to prepare and implement as part of a classroom routine, at the beginning of each mathematics lesson as a warm-up or Problem of the Day, or as homework. Students can work on the practice pages independently or in cooperative groups. The practice pages can also be utilized as diagnostic tools, formative assessments, or summative assessments, which can direct differentiated small-group instruction during Mathematics Workshop.

Domains and Practice Standards

The chart below indicates the mathematics domains addressed and practice standards applied throughout this book. The subsequent chart shows the breakdown of which mathematics standard is covered in each week.

Note: Students may not have deep understanding of some topics in this book. Remember to assess students based on their problem-solving skills and not exclusively on their content knowledge.

Grade-Level Domains	Practice Standards
1. Operations and Algebraic Thinking 2. Number and Operations in Base Ten 3. Measurement and Data 4. Geometry	1. Make sense of problems and persevere in solving them. 2. Reason abstractly and quantitatively. 3. Construct viable arguments and critique the reasoning of others. 4. Model with mathematics. 5. Use appropriate tools strategically. 6. Attend to precision. 7. Look for and make use of structure. 8. Look for and express regularity in repeated reasoning.

HOW TO USE THIS BOOK *(cont.)*

College-and-Career Readiness Standards

Below is a list of mathematical standards that are addressed throughout this book. Each week students solve problems related to the same mathematical topic.

Week(s)	Standard
1	Understand that the three digits of a three-digit number represent amounts of hundreds, tens, and ones. 100 can be thought of as a bundle of ten tens—called a "hundred." The numbers 100, 200, 300, 400, 500, 600, 700, 800, 900 refer to one, two, three, four, five, six, seven, eight, or nine hundreds (and 0 tens and 0 ones).
2	Count within 1,000; skip-count by 5s, 10s, and 100s.
3	Read and write numbers to 1,000 using base-ten numerals, number names, and expanded form.
4 and 5	Compare two three-digit numbers based on meanings of the hundreds, tens, and ones digits, using >, =, and < symbols to record the results of comparisons.
6	Fluently add and subtract within 20 using mental strategies. By end of Grade 2, know from memory all sums of two one-digit numbers.
7 and 8	Use addition within 100 to solve one-step word problems involving situations of adding to, putting together, and comparing, e.g., by using drawings and equations with a symbol for the unknown number to represent the problem.
9 and 10	Use subtraction within 100 to solve one-step word problems involving situations of taking from, taking apart, and comparing, e.g., by using drawings and equations with a symbol for the unknown number to represent the problem.
11	Use addition within 100 to solve two-step word problems involving situations of adding to, putting together, and comparing, e.g., by using drawings and equations with a symbol for the unknown number to represent the problem.
12	Use subtraction within 100 to solve two-step word problems involving situations of taking from, taking apart, and comparing, e.g., by using drawings and equations with a symbol for the unknown number to represent the problem.

HOW TO USE THIS BOOK (cont.)

Week(s)	Standard
13 and 14	Use addition and subtraction within 100 to solve one- and two-step word problems involving situations of adding to, taking from, putting together, taking apart, and comparing, e.g., by using drawings and equations with a symbol for the unknown number to represent the problem.
15	Determine whether a group of objects (up to 20) has an odd or even number of members, e.g., by pairing objects or counting them by 2s; write an equation to express an even number as a sum of two equal addends.
16 and 17	Use addition to find the total number of objects arranged in rectangular arrays with up to 5 rows and up to 5 columns; write an equation to express the total as a sum of equal addends.
18	Fluently add and subtract within 100 using strategies based on place value, properties of operations, and/or the relationship between addition and subtraction.
19	Add up to four two-digit numbers using strategies based on place value and properties of operations.
20 and 21	Add and subtract within 1,000, using concrete models or drawings and strategies based on place value, properties of operations, and/or the relationship between addition and subtraction; relate the strategy to a written method. Understand that in adding or subtracting three-digit numbers, one adds or subtracts hundreds and hundreds, tens and tens, ones and ones; and sometimes it is necessary to compose or decompose tens or hundreds.
22	Mentally add 10 or 100 to a given number 100–900, and mentally subtract 10 or 100 from a given number 100–900.
23	Explain why addition and subtraction strategies work using place value and properties of operation.
24	Measure the length of an object by selecting and using appropriate tools such as rulers, yardsticks, meter sticks, and measuring tapes.
25	Measure the length of an object twice, using length units of different lengths for the two measurements; describe how the two measurements relate to the size of the unit chosen.
26	Estimate lengths using units of inches, feet, centimeters, and meters.

HOW TO USE THIS BOOK *(cont.)*

Week(s)	Standard
27	Measure to determine how much longer one object is than another, expressing the length difference in terms of a standard length unit.
28	Use addition and subtraction within 100 to solve word problems involving lengths that are given in the same units, e.g., by using drawings (such as drawings of rulers) and equations with a symbol for the unknown number to represent the problem.
29	Represent whole numbers as lengths from 0 on a number line diagram with equally spaced points corresponding to the numbers 0, 1, 2, and represent whole-number sums and differences within 100 on a number line diagram.
30	Tell and write time from analog and digital clocks to the nearest five minutes, using a.m. and p.m.
31	Solve word problems involving dollar bills, quarters, dimes, nickels, and pennies, using $ and ¢ symbols appropriately.
32	Generate measurement data by measuring lengths of several objects to the nearest whole unit, or by making repeated measurements of the same object. Show the measurements by making a line plot, where the horizontal scale is marked off in whole-number units.
33	Draw a bar graph (with single-unit scale) to represent a data set with up to four categories. Solve simple put-together, take-apart, and compare problems using information presented in a bar graph.
34	Recognize and draw shapes having specified attributes, such as a given number of angles or a given number of equal faces. Identify triangles, quadrilaterals, pentagons, hexagons, and cubes.
35	Partition a rectangle into rows and columns of same-size squares and count to find the total number of them.
36	Partition circles and rectangles into two, three, or four equal shares, describe the shares using the words halves, thirds, half of, a third of, etc., and describe the whole as two halves, three thirds, four fourths. Recognize that equal shares of identical wholes need not have the same shape.

HOW TO USE THIS BOOK *(cont.)*

Using the Practice Pages

The activity pages provide practice and assessment opportunities for each day of the school year. Students focus on one grade-level skill each week. The five-day plan requires students to think about the problem-solving process, use visual models, choose multiple strategies, and solve multi-step, non-routine word problems. For this grade level, teachers may complete the pages together as a class, or students may work in cooperative groups. Teachers may prepare packets of weekly practice pages for the classroom or for homework.

 Day 1–Think About It!
For the first day of each week, the focus is on thinking about the problem-solving process. Students might draw pictures or answer questions about a problem. The goal is to understand the process of solving a problem more so than finding the solution.

 Day 2–Solve It!
On the second day of each week, students solve a routine problem based on the thinking process from Day 1. Students will think about the information given in the problem, decide on a plan, solve the problem, and look back and explain their work.

 Day 3–Picture It!
On day three, a visual representation (e.g., number line, table, diagram) is shown as a strategy for solving a problem. Students use this visual model to solve a similar problem.

 Day 4–Solve It Two Ways!
On the fourth day, students solve the same problem two ways by applying the strategies they have learned. Students may also be asked to analyze how others solved a problem and explain which way is correct or state the error or misconception.

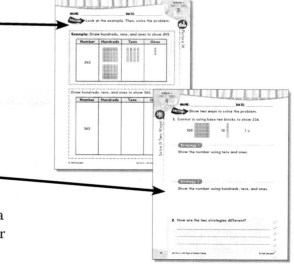

HOW TO USE THIS BOOK *(cont.)*

Day 5–Challenge Yourself!
On day five, students are presented with a multi-step, non-routine problem. Students analyze a problem, think about different strategies, develop a plan, and explain how they solved the problem.

Using the Resources

The following resources will be helpful to students as they complete the activity pages. Print copies of these resources and provide them to students to keep at their desks. These resources are available as Adobe® PDFs online. A complete list of the available documents is provided on page 219. To access the digital resources, go to this website: **http://www.tcmpub.com/download-files**. Enter this code: 91439026. Follow the on-screen directions.

Practice Page Rubric can be found on page 211 and in the Digital Resources (rubric.pdf). The rubric can be used to assess students' mathematical understanding of the weekly concept and steps in the problem-solving process. The rubric should be shared with students so they know what is expected of them.

Problem-Solving Framework can be found on page 217 and in the Digital Resources (framework.pdf). Students can reference each step of the problem-solving process as they complete the practice pages during the week.

Problem-Solving Strategies can be found on page 218 and in the Digital Resources (strategies.pdf). Students may want to reference this page when choosing strategies as they solve problems throughout the week.

HOW TO USE THIS BOOK *(cont.)*

Diagnostic Assessment

Teachers can use the practice pages as diagnostic assessments. The data analysis tools included with the book enable teachers or parents to quickly score students' work and monitor their progress. Teachers and parents can quickly see which steps in the problem-solving process students need to target further to develop proficiency.

After students complete a week of practice pages, each page can be graded using the answer key (pages 193–210). Then, the *Practice Page Rubric* (page 211; rubric.pdf) can be used to score each practice page. The *Practice Page Item Analysis* (pages 212–215; itemanalysis.pdf) can be completed. The *Practice Page Item Analysis* can be used to record students' Day 5 practice page score, while the *Student Item Analysis* (page 216; studentitem.pdf) can be used to record a student's daily practice page score. These charts are also provided in the Digital Resources as PDFs, Microsoft Word® files (itemanalysis.docx; studentitem.docx), and Microsoft Excel® files (itemanalysis.xlsx; studentitem.xlsx). Teachers can input data into the electronic files directly on the computer, or they can print the pages and analyze students' work using paper and pencil.

To Complete the Practice Page Item Analysis

- Write or type students' names in the far-left column. Depending on the number of students, more than one copy of the form may be needed, or you may need to add rows.

- The specific week is indicated across the top of each chart.

- Record rubric scores for the Day 5 practice page in the appropriate column.

- Add the scores for each student. Place that sum in the far-right column. Use these scores as benchmarks to determine how each student is performing after a nine-week period. This allows for four benchmarks during the year that can be used to gather formative diagnostic data.

HOW TO USE THIS BOOK *(cont.)*

To Complete the Student Item Analysis

- Write or type the student's name in the top row. This form tracks the ongoing process of each student, so one copy per student is necessary.
- The specific day is indicated across the top of each chart.
- Record the student's rubric score for each practice page in the appropriate column.
- Add the scores for the student. Place that sum in the far-right column. Use these scores as benchmarks to determine how the student is performing each week. These benchmarks can be used to gather formative diagnostic data.

Using the Results to Differentiate Instruction

Once results are gathered and analyzed, teachers can use the results to inform the way they differentiate instruction. The data can help determine which mathematical concepts and steps in the problem-solving process are the most difficult for students and which students need additional instructional support and continued practice.

Whole-Class Support

The results of the diagnostic analysis may show that the entire class is struggling with a particular mathematical concept or problem-solving step. If these concepts or problem-solving steps have been taught in the past, this indicates that further instruction or reteaching is necessary. If these concepts or steps have not been taught in the past, this data may indicate that students do not have a working knowledge of the concepts or steps. Thus, careful planning for the length of the unit(s) or lesson(s) must be considered, and additional front-loading may be required.

Small-Group or Individual Support

The results of the diagnostic analysis may show that an individual student or small group of students is struggling with a particular mathematical concept or problem-solving step. If these concepts or steps have been taught in the past, this indicates that further instruction or reteaching is necessary. These students can be pulled to a small group for further instruction on the concept(s) or step(s), while other students work independently. Students may also benefit from extra practice using games or computer-based resources. Teachers can also use the results to help identify individual students or groups of proficient students who are ready for enrichment or above-grade-level instruction. These groups may benefit from independent learning contracts or more challenging activities.

Digital Resources

The Digital Resources contain diagnostic pages and additional resources, such as the *Problem-Solving Framework* and *Problem-Solving Strategies* pages, for students. The list of resources in the Digital Resources can be found on page 219.

STANDARDS CORRELATIONS

Shell Education is committed to producing educational materials that are research- and standards-based. In this effort, we have correlated all of our products to the academic standards of all 50 states, the District of Columbia, the Department of Defense Dependents Schools, and all Canadian provinces.

How to Find Standards Correlations

To print a customized correlation report of this product for your state, visit our website at **http://www.tcmpub.com/shell-education**. If you require assistance in printing correlation reports, please contact our Customer Service Department at 1-877-777-3450.

Purpose and Intent of Standards

The Every Student Succeeds Act (ESSA) mandates that all states adopt challenging academic standards that help students meet the goal of college and career readiness. While many states already adopted academic standards prior to ESSA, the act continues to hold states accountable for detailed and comprehensive standards.

Standards are designed to focus instruction and guide adoption of curricula. Standards are statements that describe the criteria necessary for students to meet specific academic goals. They define the knowledge, skills, and content students should acquire at each level. Standards are also used to develop standardized tests to evaluate students' academic progress.

Teachers are required to demonstrate how their lessons meet state standards. State standards are used in the development of all of our products, so educators can be assured they meet the academic requirements of each state.

The activities in this book are aligned to today's national and state-specific college-and-career readiness standards. The chart on page 4 lists the domains and practice standards addressed throughout this book. A more detailed chart on pages 5–7 correlates the specific mathematics content standards to each week.

NAME: _____ **DATE:** _____

 DIRECTIONS: Think about the problem. Answer the questions.

Brandon is organizing bundles of craft sticks. There are 10 craft sticks in each bundle. He knows there are 300 craft sticks. How many bundles are there?

Think About It!

1. **What do you know about the problem?**

   _____

   _____

2. **What do you need to find?**

   _____

   _____

   _____

3. **How can you solve the problem?**

   _____

   _____

   _____

NAME: _____ **DATE:** _____

Solve It!

DIRECTIONS: Read and solve the problem.

Problem: Brandon is organizing bundles of craft sticks. There are 10 craft sticks in each bundle. He knows there are 300 craft sticks. How many bundles are there?

? What Do You Know?

🔑 What Is Your Plan?

💡 Solve the Problem!

🔍 Look Back and Explain!

NAME: _____ **DATE:** _____

 DIRECTIONS: Look at the example. Then, solve the problem.

Example: Draw hundreds, tens, and ones to show 243.

Number	Hundreds	Tens	Ones
243			

Draw hundreds, tens, and ones to show 365.

Number	Hundreds	Tens	Ones
365			

Solve It Two Ways!

NAME: _____ DATE: _____

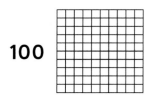 **DIRECTIONS:** Show two ways to solve the problem.

1. Connor is using base-ten blocks to show 236.

100   10   1 □

Strategy 1

Show the number using tens and ones.

Strategy 2

Show the number using hundreds, tens, and ones.

2. How are the two strategies different?

_____

_____

_____

NAME: _____ **DATE:** _____

 DIRECTIONS: Read and solve the problem.

Laura draws a picture to show a number.

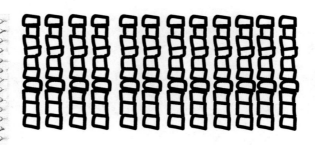

1. Show the number a different way with words, numbers, or pictures.

2. Show the number a third way with words, numbers, or pictures.

NAME: _____ **DATE:** _____

Think About It!

DIRECTIONS: Think about the problem. Answer the questions.

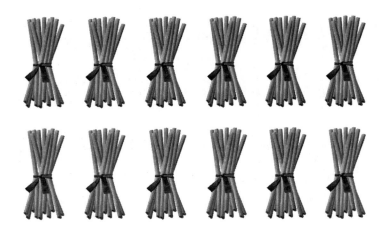

There are 10 straws in each bundle. Count the straws by tens. How many straws are there?

1. What do you know about the problem?

_____

_____

2. What do you need to find?

_____

_____

_____

3. How can you solve the problem?

_____

_____

_____

NAME: _____ **DATE:** _____

 DIRECTIONS: Read and solve the problem.

Problem: There are 10 straws in each bundle. Count the straws by tens. How many straws are there?

? What Do You Know?

🔑 What Is Your Plan?

💡 Solve the Problem!

🔍 Look Back and Explain!

NAME: _____ **DATE:** _____

Picture It!

DIRECTIONS: Look at the example. Then, solve the problem.

Example: Count by fives. Write the numbers on the number line.

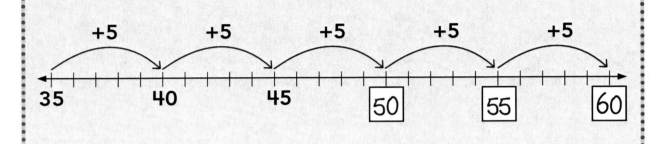

Count by twos. Write the numbers on the number line.

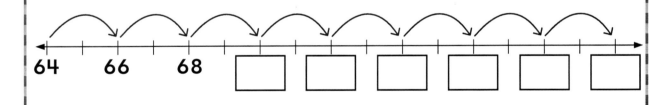

NAME: _____ **DATE:** _____

DIRECTIONS: Show two ways to solve the problem.

Solve It Two Ways!

1. How many flowers are there?

.... **Strategy 1** ....

Count the flowers by ones. Write the numbers.

___ ___ ___ ___ ___ ___ ___ ___ ___ ___ ___

___ ___ ___ ___ ___ ___ ___ ___ ___ ___ ___

___ ___ ___ ___ ___ ___ ___ ___ ___

___ ___ ___ ___ ___ ___

.... **Strategy 2** ....

Count the flowers by fives. Write the numbers.

___ ___ ___ ___ ___ ___ ___ ___

2. Which strategy do you think is easier? Explain your reasoning.

_____

_____

_____

NAME: _____ DATE: _____

DIRECTIONS: Read and solve the problem.

Complete the hundreds chart. Then, use the chart to count.

Challenge Yourself!

1	2	3	4		6	7	8	9	
11	12	13	14	15	16	17		19	20
21	22	23		25	26	27	28	29	
31		33	34		36	37		39	40
41	42	43				47		49	
51			54	55	56		58		60
	62		64	65	66			69	
71	72	73	74		76			79	80
	82		84		86			89	90
		93	94		96	97		99	100

1. Use the chart to count by tens. Color the numbers yellow. Write about the pattern.

   _____

   _____

2. Use the chart to count by fives. Color the numbers blue. Write about the pattern.

   _____

   _____

NAME: _____ **DATE:** _____

 DIRECTIONS: Think about the problem. Answer the questions.

Juan says the number in his home address is six hundred fifty-eight. What numbers should Juan write to show his address?

1. **What do you know about the problem?**

   _____

   _____

2. **What do you need to find?**

   _____

   _____

   _____

3. **How can you solve the problem?**

   _____

   _____

   _____

Solve It!

NAME: _____ DATE: _____

DIRECTIONS: Read and solve the problem.

Problem: Juan says the number in his home address is six hundred fifty-eight. What numbers should Juan write to show his address?

? What Do You Know?

🔑 What Is Your Plan?

💡 Solve the Problem!

🔍 Look Back and Explain!

#51614—180 Days of Problem Solving

© Shell Education

NAME: _____ **DATE:** _____

DIRECTIONS: Look at the example. Then, solve the problem.

Example: Look at the base-ten blocks. Write the number of hundreds, tens, and ones.

__3__ hundreds __5__ tens __4__ ones

The number is __354__ .

Look at the base-ten blocks. Write the number of hundreds, tens, and ones.

_____ hundreds _____ tens ____ ones

The number is _____ .

Solve It Two Ways!

NAME: _____ DATE: _____

DIRECTIONS: Show two ways to solve the problem.

1. There are eight hundred forty-two students at Cleveland Elementary School. What are two other ways to write this number?

Strategy 1

Expanded form:

_____ + _____ + _____

Strategy 2

Number form:

_____

2. How are the two strategies different?

_____

_____

_____

#51614—180 Days of Problem Solving   © Shell Education

NAME: _____ **DATE:** _____

 DIRECTIONS: Read and solve the problem.

Look at the base-ten blocks. Write the number three different ways.

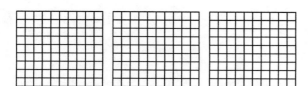

1. **Expanded form:**

   _____

   _____

2. **Word form:**

   _____

   _____

3. **Number form:**

   _____

   _____

Think About It!

NAME: _____ DATE: _____

DIRECTIONS: Think about the problem. Answer the questions.

Rhys wants to compare the numbers 624 and 608. How can he use >, <, or = to compare the numbers?

624 ◯ 608

1. **What do you know about the problem?**

_____

_____

2. **What do you need to find?**

_____

_____

_____

3. **How can you solve the problem?**

_____

_____

_____

_____

NAME: _____ **DATE:** _____

 **DIRECTIONS:** Read and solve the problem.

Problem: Rhys wants to compare the numbers 624 and 608. How can he use >, <, or = to compare the numbers?

 **What Do You Know?**

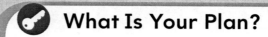 **What Is Your Plan?**

 **Solve the Problem!**

◯ _____ _____

 **Look Back and Explain!**

Picture It!

NAME: _____ DATE: _____

DIRECTIONS: Look at the example. Then, solve the problem by drawing base-ten blocks.

Example: Which number is greater? Use >, <, or = to compare the numbers.

316 (>) 314

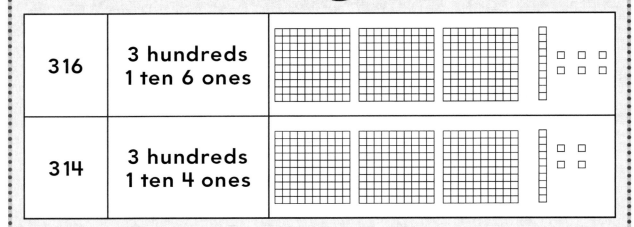

| 316 | 3 hundreds 1 ten 6 ones | |
| 314 | 3 hundreds 1 ten 4 ones | |

_316_ is greater.

Which number is less? Use >, <, or = to compare the numbers.

230 ( ) 207

| 230 | 2 hundreds 3 tens 0 ones | |
| 207 | 2 hundreds 0 tens 7 ones | |

_____ is less.

NAME: _____ DATE: _____

 DIRECTIONS: Show two ways to solve the problem.

1. Two panda bears live at the zoo. One bear weighs 215 pounds. The other bear weighs 245 pounds. Which panda bear weighs more?

· · · · **Strategy 1** ·

Draw base-ten blocks to show each number. Circle the number that is greater.

       215   245

· · · · **Strategy 2** ·

Write each number in expanded form. Use >, <, or = to compare the numbers.

_____ + _____ + _____ ◯ _____ + _____ + _____

2. Which strategy do you think is better? Explain your reasoning.

_____

_____

_____

Challenge Yourself!

NAME: _____ **DATE:** _____

DIRECTIONS: Read and solve the problem.

Use the numbers in the squares to write three comparisons. You may use the numbers more than once.

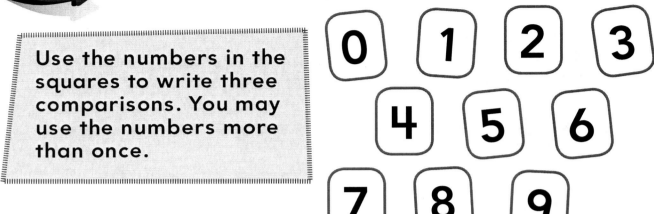

1. ☐ ☐ ☐ > ☐ ☐ ☐

2. ☐ ☐ ☐ < ☐ ☐ ☐

3. ☐ ☐ ☐ = ☐ ☐ ☐

4. What strategy helped you write your comparisons? Explain your thinking.

_____

_____

_____

_____

NAME: _____ **DATE:** _____

 DIRECTIONS: Think about the problem. Answer the questions.

Mr. Rios has two cows on his farm. One cow weighs 732 pounds. Another cow weighs 832 pounds. Compare the weights using >, <, or =.

100   10   1

Think About It!

---

1. What do you know about the problem?

_____

_____

2. What do you need to find?

_____

_____

3. How many hundreds, tens, and ones are in 732 and 832?

732 = _____ hundreds _____ tens _____ ones

832 = _____ hundreds _____ tens _____ ones

Solve It!

NAME: _____ DATE: _____

DIRECTIONS: Read and solve the problem.

Problem: Mr. Rios has two cows on his farm. One cow weighs 732 pounds. Another cow weighs 832 pounds. Compare the weights using >, <, or =.

? **What Do You Know?**

⚷ **What Is Your Plan?**

💡 **Solve the Problem!**

_____ ⭘ _____

🔍 **Look Back and Explain!**

NAME: _____ **DATE:** _____

 DIRECTIONS: Look at the example. Then, solve the problem.

Picture It!

Example: A sheep's weight in pounds is shown with base-ten blocks. What is the weight in number form?

__2__ hundreds __4__ tens __5__ ones

__245__ pounds

A horse's weight in pounds is shown with base-ten blocks. What is the weight in number form?

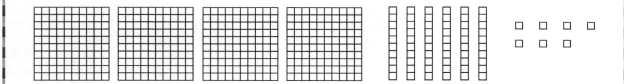

_____ hundreds _____ tens _____ ones

_____ pounds

#51614—180 Days of Problem Solving

NAME: _____ **DATE:** _____

Solve It Two Ways!

DIRECTIONS: Show two ways to solve the problem.

1. Mr. Rios wants to buy a pig. He wants the weight of the pig to be greater than 225 pounds, but less than 250 pounds. What are two possible weights of the pig?

Solution 1

Solution 2

2. Use place value to explain how you found two solutions to the problem.

_____

_____

_____

NAME: _____ DATE: _____

 DIRECTIONS: Read and solve the problem.

Mr. Rios has a greater number of acres on his farm than Mr. Gonzalez. Use the numbers in the squares to compare Mr. Rios's acres to Mr. Gonzalez's acres. Use each number only once.

1. Compare Mr. Rios's number of acres to Mr. Gonzalez's number of acres.

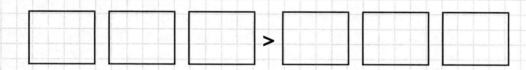

2. Use the numbers you wrote to write a story problem.

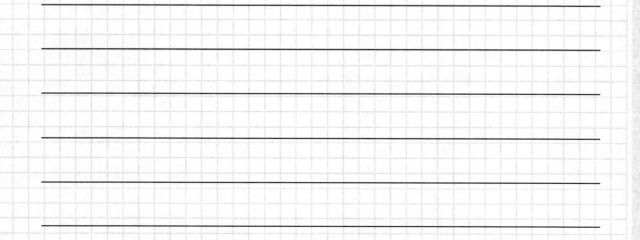

Think About It!

NAME: _____ **DATE:** _____

DIRECTIONS: Think about the problem. Answer the questions.

The numbers 9, 4, and 13 belong to a fact family. What two addition sentences can these numbers make? What two subtraction sentences can these numbers make?

1. What do you know about the problem?

_____

_____

2. What do you need to find?

_____

_____

_____

3. How can you solve the problem?

_____

_____

_____

NAME: _____ **DATE:** _____

 DIRECTIONS: Read and solve the problem.

Problem: The numbers 9, 4, and 13 belong to a fact family. What two addition sentences can these numbers make? What two subtraction sentences can these numbers make?

? What Do You Know?

🔑 What Is Your Plan?

💡 Solve the Problem!

_____ + _____ = _____

_____ + _____ = _____

_____ – _____ = _____

_____ – _____ = _____

🔍 Look Back and Explain!

Picture It!

NAME: _____ **DATE:** _____

DIRECTIONS: Look at the example. Then, solve the problem using ten frames.

Example: Caroline has 8 marbles. Todd has 9 marbles. How many marbles do they have in all?

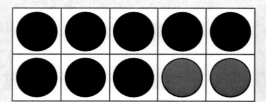 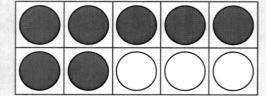

____17____ marbles

Joey has 6 toy trucks. Jasmine has 7 toy trucks. How many toy trucks do they have in all?

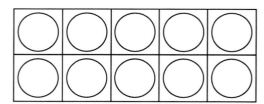 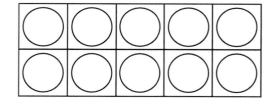

_____ toy trucks

NAME: _____ DATE: _____

DIRECTIONS: Show two ways to solve the problem.

1. Josie has 13 stickers. She gives 5 stickers to her brother. How many stickers does Josie have now?

Strategy 1

Use the ten frames to solve the problem.

Strategy 2

Count back from 13 to solve the problem.

13 _____ _____ _____ _____ _____

2. Which strategy do you think is easier? Explain your reasoning.

_____

_____

_____

NAME: _____ **DATE:** _____

DIRECTIONS: Read and solve the problem.

Complete the addition table to show the sums.

+	1	2	3	4	5	6	7	8	9	10
1										
2										
3										
4										
5										
6										
7										
8										
9										
10										

How can you use this table to solve addition problems?

_____

_____

_____

_____

_____

_____

NAME: _____ **DATE:** _____

DIRECTIONS: Think about the problem. Answer the questions.

Jack has 13 blue blocks and 14 green blocks. How many blocks does Jack have in all?

1. **What do you know about the problem?**

_____

_____

2. **What do you need to find?**

_____

_____

3. **Draw base-ten blocks to show each number.**

13	14

Solve It!

NAME: _____ **DATE:** _____

DIRECTIONS: Read and solve the problem.

Problem: Jack has 13 blue blocks and 14 green blocks. How many blocks does Jack have in all?

 What Do You Know?

What Is Your Plan?

 Solve the Problem!

 Look Back and Explain!

NAME: _____ **DATE:** _____

 DIRECTIONS: Look at the example. Then, solve the problem using a number line.

Example: Jasper has 16 red marbles and 5 purple marbles. How many marbles does he have in all? Write a number sentence to show the answer.

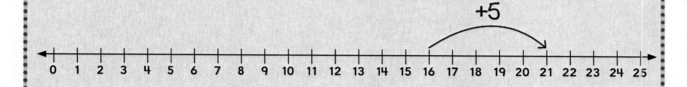

$$\underline{16 + 5 = 21}$$

Jessica has 12 red marbles and 7 purple marbles. How many marbles does she have in all? Write a number sentence to show the answer.

_____

Solve It Two Ways!

NAME: _____ DATE: _____

DIRECTIONS: Show two ways to solve the problem.

1. Sophia has 26 red crayons. She has 12 blue crayons. How many crayons does Sophia have altogether?

   Strategy 1

   Use the ten frames to solve the problem.

   Strategy 2

   Start with 26 and count on to solve the problem.

   26 _____ _____ _____ _____

   _____ _____ _____ _____

   _____ _____ _____ _____

2. Which strategy do you think is easier? Explain your reasoning.

   _____

   _____

   _____

NAME: _____ **DATE:** _____

 DIRECTIONS: Read and solve the problem.

Anthony has some yellow markers and some red markers. Use the numbers in the squares to write an addition sentence. Use each number only once.

1. **What addition sentence can you write?**

2. **Use your number sentence to write a story problem about Anthony and his markers.**

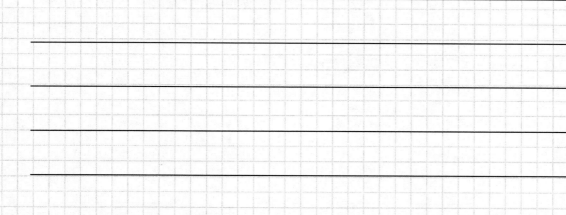

Think About It!

NAME: _____ **DATE:** _____

DIRECTIONS: Think about the problem. Answer the questions.

Dominic and his mother make 25 cookies for his birthday party. Then, they make 23 more cookies. How many cookies did Dominic and his mother make?

1. What do you know about the problem?

_____

_____

2. What do you need to find?

_____

_____

_____

3. How can you solve the problem?

_____

_____

_____

NAME: _____ **DATE:** _____

 DIRECTIONS: Read and solve the problem.

Problem: Dominic and his mother make 25 cookies for his birthday party. Then, they make 23 more cookies. How many cookies did Dominic and his mother make?

Solve It!

? What Do You Know?

🔑 What Is Your Plan?

💡 Solve the Problem!

🔍 Look Back and Explain!

Picture It!

NAME: _____ **DATE:** _____

DIRECTIONS: Look at the example. Then, solve the problem using a number line.

Example: Dominic's mother buys 12 books and 7 puzzles to give to the children at his birthday party. How many gifts does his mother buy? Write a number sentence to show the answer.

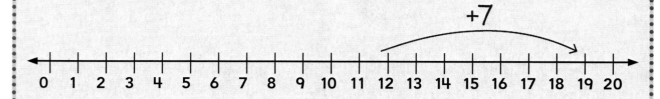

$$12 + 7 = 19$$

Dominic invites 9 boys and 8 girls to his party. How many children does he invite? Write a number sentence to show the answer.

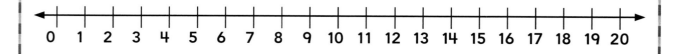

_____

NAME: _____ **DATE:** _____

DIRECTIONS: Show two ways to solve the problem.

1. Dominic has 11 blue party hats. He has 18 red party hats. How many party hats are there in all?

Strategy 1

Count on from 18 to find the total.

18 _____ _____ _____ _____

_____ _____ _____ _____

_____ _____ _____

Strategy 2

Use the ten frames to find the total.

2. Which strategy do you think is easier? Explain your reasoning.

_____

_____

_____

Challenge Yourself!

NAME: _____ **DATE:** _____

DIRECTIONS: Read and solve the problem.

At Dominic's party, the children play games. Then, they watch a puppet show. Use the numbers in the squares to write an addition sentence for the number of minutes the children play games and watch a puppet show. You may use the numbers more than once.

1. What addition sentence can you write?

2. Use your addition sentence to write a story problem about the number of minutes the children play games and watch a puppet show.

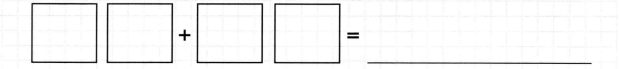

_____

_____

_____

_____

_____

_____

NAME: _____ **DATE:** _____

 DIRECTIONS: Think about the problem. Answer the questions.

Olivia scores 89 points on a video game. She plays again and scores 57 points. What is the difference between the points she scores on the two games?

Think About It!

1. What do you know about the problem?

_____

_____

2. What do you need to find?

_____

_____

_____

3. How can you solve the problem?

_____

_____

_____

Solve It!

NAME: _____ **DATE:** _____

 Read and solve the problem.

Problem: Olivia scores 89 points on a video game. She plays again and scores 57 points. What is the difference between the points she scores on the two games?

 What Do You Know?

What Is Your Plan?

Solve the Problem!

 **Look Back and Explain!**

NAME: _____ DATE: _____

 DIRECTIONS: Look at the example. Then, solve the problem using a number line.

Picture It!

Example: Audrey scores 64 points on a video game. She plays again and scores 43 points. How many more points does she score in her first game?

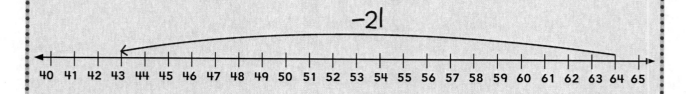

$$64 - 43 = 21$$

Monica scores 63 points on a video game. She plays again and scores fewer points. The difference between the points is 22. How many points does she score in her second game?

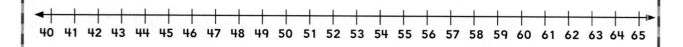

_____

NAME: _____ **DATE:** _____

Solve It Two Ways!

DIRECTIONS: Show two ways to solve the problem.

1. The sum of the points Brianna scores on two video games is 43 points. She scores 21 points on the second video game. How many points does Brianna score on the first video game?

Strategy 1

Use the number line to solve the problem.

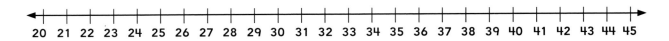

20 21 22 23 24 25 26 27 28 29 30 31 32 33 34 35 36 37 38 39 40 41 42 43 44 45

Strategy 2

Count back from 43 to 21 to solve the problem.

43 _____ _____ _____ _____ _____ _____

_____ _____ _____ _____ _____ _____

_____ _____ _____ _____ _____ _____

_____ _____ _____ _____

2. Which strategy do you think is easier? Explain your reasoning.

_____

_____

_____

NAME: _____ **DATE:** _____

 DIRECTIONS: Read and solve the problem.

Jamie is playing two video games. Use the numbers in the squares to write a subtraction sentence to show the difference between her scores on the two games. Use each number only once.

1. What number sentence can you write?

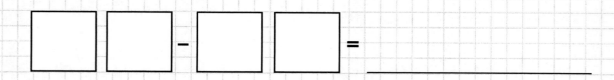

2. Use your number sentence to write a story problem about Jamie and her scores on the two video games.

_____

_____

_____

_____

_____

Think About It!

NAME: _____ **DATE:** _____

DIRECTIONS: Think about the problem. Answer the questions.

In Mr. Sullivan's library, there are 87 books. He finds 23 books about dinosaurs. Write a subtraction sentence to show how many books are **not** about dinosaurs.

1. What do you know about the problem?

   _____

   _____

2. What do you need to find?

   _____

   _____

3. Draw a picture using base-ten blocks to show the problem.

NAME: _____ DATE: _____

 **DIRECTIONS:** Read and solve the problem.

Problem: In Mr. Sullivan's library, there are 87 books. He finds 23 books about dinosaurs. Write a subtraction sentence to show how many books are **not** about dinosaurs.

 What Do You Know?

 What Is Your Plan?

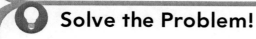 **Solve the Problem!**

 **Look Back and Explain!**

NAME: _____ **DATE:** _____

Picture It!

DIRECTIONS: Look at the example. Then, solve the problem using a number line.

Example: In Mr. Lee's library, there are 37 books about space. Paula has read 22 of them. How many more books about space can Paula read?

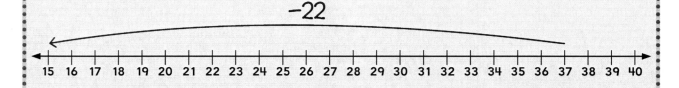

$$37 - 22 = 15$$

In Miss Robinson's library, there are 19 books about animals. Jeff has read 16 of them. How many more books about animals can Jeff read?

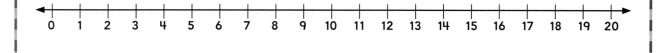

_____

NAME: _____ **DATE:** _____

DIRECTIONS: Show two ways to solve the problem.

1. In Ms. Johan's library, there are 19 books about animals and 8 books about plants. How many more books are about animals than about plants?

Strategy 1

Use ten frames to solve the problem.

Strategy 2

Count back from 19 to 8 to solve the problem.

19 _____ _____ _____ _____ _____ _____

_____ _____ _____ _____ _____

2. Which strategy do you think is easier? Explain your reasoning.

_____

_____

_____

Challenge Yourself!

NAME: _____ DATE: _____

DIRECTIONS: Read and solve the problem.

In Ms. Bing's library, there are fiction books and nonfiction books. Use the numbers in the squares to write a subtraction sentence to show the difference between the number of fiction books and the number of nonfiction books. Use each number only once.

1. What number sentence can you write?

2. Use your number sentence to write a story problem about the number of fiction books and nonfiction books in Ms. Bing's library.

_____

_____

_____

_____

NAME: _____ **DATE:** _____

DIRECTIONS: Think about the problem. Answer the questions.

Emily owns a bakery. On Monday, she sells 34 cupcakes. On Tuesday, she sells 42 cupcakes. On Wednesday, she sells 21 more cupcakes. How many cupcakes does Emily sell on these three days?

1. What do you know about the problem?

_____

_____

2. What do you need to find?

_____

_____

_____

3. How can you solve the problem?

_____

_____

_____

Solve It!

NAME: _____ DATE: _____

DIRECTIONS: Read and solve the problem.

Problem: Emily owns a bakery. On Monday, she sells 34 cupcakes. On Tuesday, she sells 42 cupcakes. On Wednesday, she sells 21 more cupcakes. How many cupcakes does Emily sell on these three days?

? What Do You Know?

🔑 What Is Your Plan?

💡 Solve the Problem!

🔍 Look Back and Explain!

NAME: _____ DATE: _____

DIRECTIONS: Look at the example. Then, solve the problem using a number line.

Example: On Friday, Emily's bakery had 15 customers. On Saturday, it had 22 customers. On Sunday, it had 11 more customers. How many customers came to Emily's bakery on these three days?

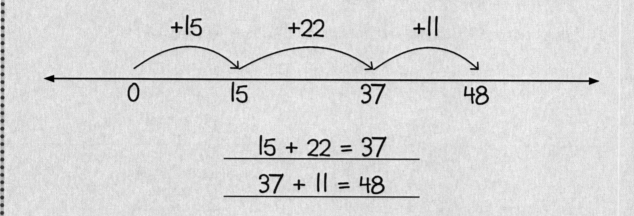

$$15 + 22 = 37$$
$$37 + 11 = 48$$

On Thursday morning, Emily's bakery had 13 customers. In the afternoon, it had 14 customers. In the evening, it had 10 more customers. How many customers came to Emily's bakery on Thursday?

_____

_____

NAME: _____ **DATE:** _____

Solve It Two Ways!

DIRECTIONS: Show two ways to solve the problem.

1. Emily needs 16 eggs to make cookies. She needs 32 eggs to make cupcakes. She needs 11 eggs to make pies. How many eggs does Emily need to make the cookies, cupcakes, and pies?

Strategy 1

Use the number line to solve the problem.

$\longleftrightarrow$

Strategy 2

Use a different strategy to solve the problem.

2. Which strategy do you think is easier? Explain your reasoning.

_____

_____

_____

　© Shell Education

NAME: _____ **DATE:** _____

DIRECTIONS: Read and solve the problem.

On Tuesday, Emily sells some vanilla cupcakes, chocolate cupcakes, and lemon cupcakes. She sells a total of 98 cupcakes. Use six of the numbers in the squares to write an addition sentence that shows the total cupcakes Emily sells on Tuesday. Use each number only once.

1. **What number sentence can you write?**

 = 98

2. **Show your work to prove your number sentence is true.**

NAME: _____ **DATE:** _____

DIRECTIONS: Think about the problem. Answer the questions.

The students at Roosevelt Elementary had a paper airplane contest. Karen's airplane flew 39 feet. Leslie's airplane flew 11 feet less than Karen's airplane. Cheryl's airplane flew 6 feet less than Leslie's airplane. How far did Cheryl's airplane fly?

1. What do you know about the problem?

_____

_____

_____

2. What do you need to find?

_____

_____

3. How can you solve the problem?

_____

_____

_____

NAME: _____ **DATE:** _____

 DIRECTIONS: Read and solve the problem.

Problem: The students at Roosevelt Elementary had a paper airplane contest. Karen's airplane flew 39 feet. Leslie's airplane flew 11 feet less than Karen's airplane. Cheryl's airplane flew 6 feet less than Leslie's airplane. How far did Cheryl's airplane fly?

 What Do You Know?

What Is Your Plan?

Solve the Problem!

Look Back and Explain!

Picture It!

NAME: _____ **DATE:** _____

DIRECTIONS: Look at the example. Then, solve the problem using a number line.

Example: Mr. Romero's class had a paper airplane contest. Peter's airplane flew 57 inches. Andrew's airplane flew 23 inches less than Peter's airplane. Mark's airplane flew 12 inches less than Andrew's airplane. How far did Mark's airplane fly?

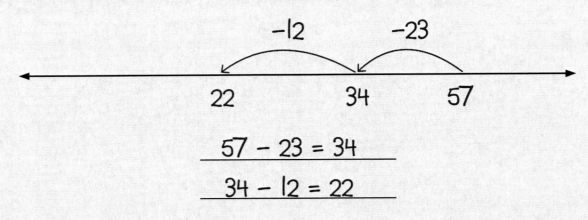

$$57 - 23 = 34$$
$$34 - 12 = 22$$

In Mr. Alba's class, Lori's airplane flew 46 inches. Stacy's airplane flew 13 inches less than Lori's airplane. Juana's airplane flew 10 inches less than Stacy's airplane. How far did Juana's airplane fly?

_____

_____

NAME: _____ **DATE:** _____

DIRECTIONS: Show two ways to solve the problem.

1. Noah's paper airplane flew 76 inches. Dylan's airplane flew 21 less inches than Noah's airplane. Connor's airplane flew 24 less inches than Dylan's airplane. How far did Connor's airplane fly?

····· **Strategy 1** ·····································

Use the number line to solve the problem.

←——————————————————————————————→

····· **Strategy 2** ·····································

Use a different strategy to solve the problem.

2. Which strategy do you like better? Explain your reasoning.

_____

_____

_____

Challenge Yourself!

NAME: _____ **DATE:** _____

DIRECTIONS: Read and solve the problem.

Archie, Daisy, and Peyton threw their paper airplanes. Daisy's airplane flew fewer inches than Archie's airplane. Peyton's airplane flew fewer inches than Daisy's airplane. Use six of the numbers in the squares to write a subtraction sentence about how far Peyton's airplane flew. You may use the numbers more than once.

1. **What number sentence can you write?**

2. **Show your work to prove your number sentence is true.**

NAME: _____ DATE: _____

 DIRECTIONS: Think about the problem. Answer the questions.

Mr. Lewis's class is learning about animals. They learned these facts.

• A pig can run 11 miles per hour.	• A squirrel can run 9 miles per hour faster than a pig.	• A mouse can run 12 miles per hour slower than a squirrel.

How fast can a squirrel run? How fast can a mouse run?

1. What do you know about the problem?

_____

_____

2. What do you need to find?

_____

_____

3. How can you solve the problem?

_____

_____

_____

Solve It!

NAME: _____ **DATE:** _____

 Read and solve the problem.

Problem: Mr. Lewis's class is learning about animals. They learned these facts.

- A pig can run 11 miles per hour.

- A squirrel can run 9 miles per hour faster than a pig.

- A mouse can run 12 miles per hour slower than a squirrel.

How fast can a squirrel run? How fast can a mouse run?

 What Do You Know?

What Is Your Plan?

 Solve the Problem!

Look Back and Explain!

NAME: _____ DATE: _____

DIRECTIONS: Look at the example. Then, solve the problem using a number line.

Picture It!

Example: A giraffe can run 32 miles per hour. An elephant runs 8 miles per hour slower than a giraffe. A zebra runs 16 miles faster than an elephant. How fast can a zebra run?

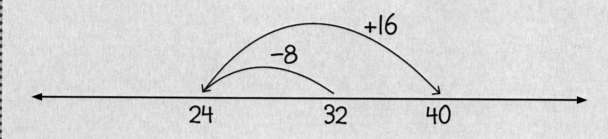

$$32 - 8 = 24$$
$$24 + 16 = 40$$

A wild dog can run 70 miles per hour. A deer can run 40 miles per hour slower than a wild dog. A squirrel can run 10 miles per hour slower than deer. How fast can a squirrel run?

⟵――――――――――――――――――――――――⟶

_____

_____

NAME: _____ **DATE:** _____

Solve It Two Ways!

DIRECTIONS: Show two ways to solve the problem.

1. A fox can run 42 miles per hour. An elk can run 45 miles per hour. An ostrich can run is 40 miles per hour. How much faster is the combined speed of a fox and an elk than an ostrich?

    Strategy 1

    Use the number line to solve the problem.

    <————————————————————————————————————>

    Strategy 2

    Use a different strategy to solve the problem.

2. Which strategy do you think is easier? Explain your reasoning.

    _____

    _____

    _____

NAME: _____ **DATE:** _____

 DIRECTIONS: Read and solve the problem.

A lion can run 54 miles per hour. It runs 12 miles per hour faster than a coyote. What is the combined speed of the lion and the coyote?

1. Write a number sentence to show how fast a coyote can run.

   _____

2. Write a number sentence to show the combined speed of the lion and the coyote.

   _____

3. Show how you found the combined speed of the lion and the coyote.

Think About It!

NAME: _____ **DATE:** _____

DIRECTIONS: Think about the problem. Answer the questions.

On Saturday, there were 55 visitors at City Zoo. On Sunday, there were 22 fewer visitors than on Saturday. How many total visitors were there on Saturday and Sunday?

1. What do you know about the problem?

_____

_____

2. What do you need to find?

_____

_____

_____

3. How can you solve the problem?

_____

_____

_____

NAME: _____ **DATE:** _____

 DIRECTIONS: Read and solve the problem.

Problem: On Saturday, there were 55 visitors at City Zoo. On Sunday, there were 22 fewer visitors than on Saturday. How many total visitors were there on Saturday and Sunday?

 What Do You Know?

What Is Your Plan?

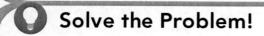 **Solve the Problem!**

 **Look Back and Explain!**

Picture It!

NAME: _____ DATE: _____

DIRECTIONS: Look at the example. Then, solve the problem using ten frames.

Example: The Fisher family is 56 miles from the aquarium. They drive 21 miles and stop. Then, they drive 26 miles. How many more miles do they need to drive to get to the aquarium?

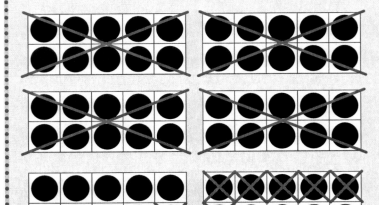

$56 - 21 = 35$

$35 - 26 = 9$

The Gomez family is 49 miles away from the museum. They drive 16 miles and stop. Then, they drive 23 miles. How many more miles do they need to drive to get to the museum?

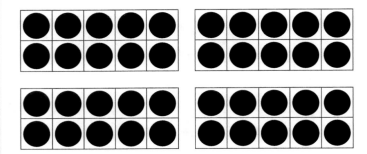

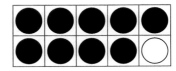

_____

_____

NAME: _____ DATE: _____

DIRECTIONS: Show two ways to solve the problem.

1. There are 25 students in a second-grade class and 24 students in another second-grade class. There are 23 students in a third-grade class and 26 students in another third-grade class. How many more students are in second grade than in third grade?

Strategy 1

Use the ten frames to solve the problem.

Strategy 2

Use a different strategy to solve the problem.

2. Which strategy do you think is easier? Explain your reasoning.

_____

_____

_____

Challenge Yourself!

NAME: _____ **DATE:** _____

DIRECTIONS: Read and solve the problem.

Students in three second-grade classes are going on a field trip. There are a total of 88 students. Use six of the numbers in the squares to write an addition sentence that tells about the problem. You may use the numbers more than once.

1. What number sentence can you write?

$$\square\square + \square\square + \square\square = 88$$

2. Show your work to prove your number sentence is true.

NAME: _____ **DATE:** _____

DIRECTIONS: Think about the problem. Answer the questions.

Each clown is holding 2 balloons. How many balloons are there?

1. What do you know about the problem?

_____

_____

2. What do you need to find?

_____

_____

3. How can you count the balloons?

_____

_____

_____

Solve It!

NAME: _____ **DATE:** _____

DIRECTIONS: Read and solve the problem.

Problem: Each clown is holding 2 balloons. Count the balloons by twos. As you count write the number. How many balloons are there?

___ ___ ___ ___ ___ ___ ___ ___

? What Do You Know?

🔑 What Is Your Plan?

💡 Solve the Problem!

____ ____ ____ ____

____ ____ ____ ____

🔍 Look Back and Explain!

NAME: _____ **DATE:** _____

DIRECTIONS: Look at the example. Then, solve the problem.

Example: Count the shapes by twos.

How many triangles are there? _____14_____

Is this number even or odd? ____even____

Explain your thinking.

There are 7 groups of 2 with 0 left over.

Count the shapes by twos.

How many squares are there? _____

Is this number even or odd? _____

Explain your thinking.

_____

Solve It Two Ways!

NAME: _____ DATE: _____

DIRECTIONS: Show two ways to solve the problem.

1. Is 18 an even number or an odd number?

Strategy 1

Draw a picture to show your answer.

Strategy 2

Count by twos. Write the numbers as you count.

_____ _____ _____ _____ _____

_____ _____ _____ _____

2. Which strategy do you think is easier? Explain your reasoning.

_____

_____

_____

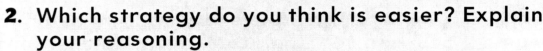

NAME: _____ DATE: _____

 DIRECTIONS: Read and solve the problem.

1. Write two even numbers that will make each number sentence true.

☐ + ☐ = 12

☐ + ☐ = 4

☐ + ☐ = 8

Number	20	17
2. Is the number even or odd?		
3. Use words, numbers, or pictures to show your thinking.		

Challenge Yourself!

Think About It!

NAME: _____ **DATE:** _____

DIRECTIONS: Think about the problem. Answer the questions.

Damien arranges his stickers in an array. There are 3 rows. There are 5 butterflies in each row. How many stickers does Damien have?

1. What do you know about the problem?

_____

_____

_____

2. What do you need to find?

_____

_____

_____

3. How can you use the array to solve the problem?

_____

_____

_____

NAME: _____ DATE: _____

 DIRECTIONS: Read and solve the problem.

Problem: Damien arranges his stickers in an array. There are 3 rows. There are 5 butterflies in each row. How many stickers does Damien have?

 What Do You Know?

 What Is Your Plan?

 Solve the Problem!

 Look Back and Explain!

Picture It!

NAME: _____ **DATE:** _____

DIRECTIONS: Look at the example. Then, solve the problem.

Example: Daniel arranges his toy cars in an array. There are 2 rows. There are 4 toy cars in each row. How many toy cars does Daniel have in his collection? Write a number sentence to show the problem.

$$\boxed{4} + \boxed{4} = \boxed{8}$$

Daniel has _____8_____ toy cars.

Lynette and her mother are making cookies. The cookies are arranged in an array. There are 5 cookies in each row. How many cookies are on the baking sheet? Write a number sentence to show the problem.

$$\boxed{} + \boxed{} = \boxed{}$$

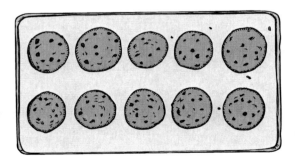

There are _____ cookies.

NAME: _____ **DATE:** _____

 DIRECTIONS: Show two ways to solve the problem.

1. Victoria likes to draw rainbows. How many rainbows does she draw?

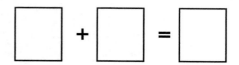 **Strategy 1**

Write a number sentence to solve the problem.

☐ + ☐ = ☐

Strategy 2

Write a different number sentence to solve the problem.

☐ + ☐ + ☐ = ☐

2. How are the two strategies different? How are they the same?

_____

_____

_____

Challenge Yourself!

NAME: _____ **DATE:** _____

Read and solve the problem.

Make four different arrays that each have a total of 12 objects. Write a number sentence for each array.

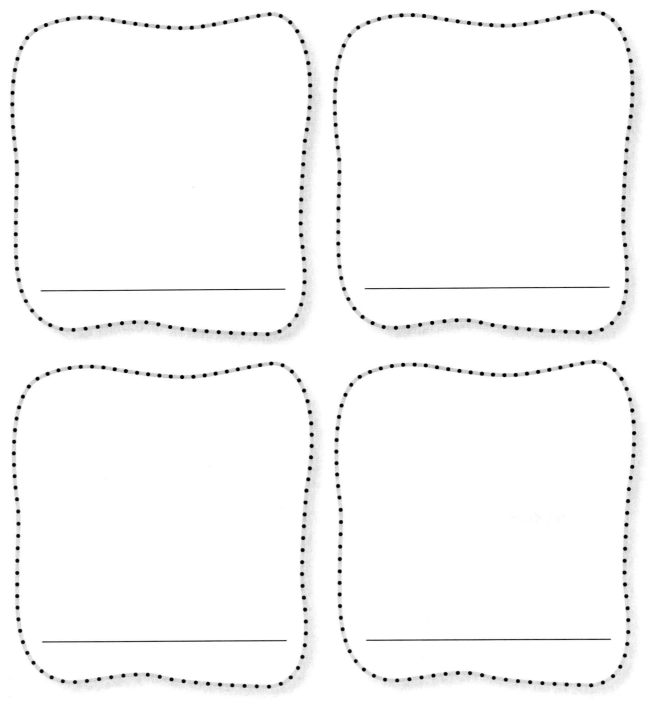

NAME: _____ **DATE:** _____

DIRECTIONS: Think about the problem. Answer the questions.

The desks in Ms. Johnson's classroom are arranged in rows. There are 5 rows. There are 5 desks in each row. How many desks are in Ms. Johnson's classroom?

1. What do you know about the problem?

_____

_____

2. What do you need to find?

_____

_____

_____

3. How can you use an array to solve the problem?

_____

_____

_____

NAME: _____ **DATE:** _____

DIRECTIONS: Read and solve the problem.

Solve It!

Problem: The desks in Ms. Johnson's classroom are arranged in rows. There are 5 rows. There are 5 desks in each row. How many desks are in Ms. Johnson's classroom?

? **What Do You Know?**

🔑 **What Is Your Plan?**

💡 **Solve the Problem!**

🔍 **Look Back and Explain!**

NAME: _____ DATE: _____

 DIRECTIONS: Look at the example. Then, solve the problem by drawing an array.

Picture It!

Example: Michelle arranges 9 coins in an array. How many equal rows of coins does she have?

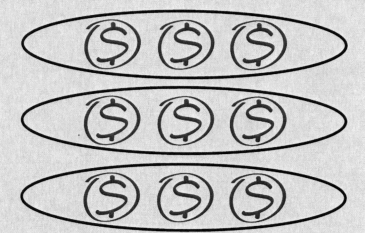

3 + 3 + 3 = 9

Michael arranges 10 coins in an array. How many equal rows of coins does he have?

_____

Solve It Two Ways!

NAME: _____ **DATE:** _____

DIRECTIONS: Show two ways to solve the problem.

1. Sandra arranges 15 cupcakes on a platter. There are the same number of cupcakes in each row. How many rows of cupcakes are there? How many cupcakes are in each row?

Strategy 1

Draw an array to solve the problem.

Strategy 2

Write a number sentence to solve the problem.

_____

2. How are the two strategies different? How are they the same?

_____

_____

_____

NAME: _____ **DATE:** _____

 DIRECTIONS: Read and solve the problem.

Kelly arranges 24 crackers on a platter. How can she arrange the crackers in equal rows? Make four different arrays. Write an addition sentence for each array.

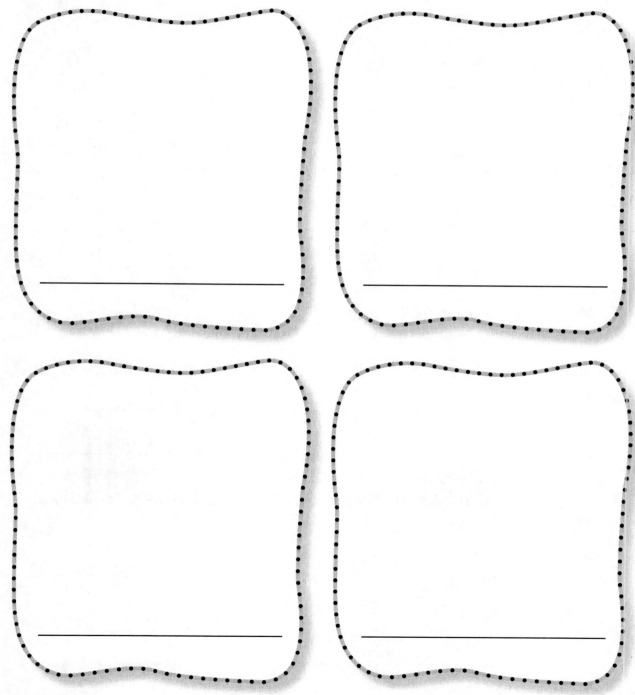

_____

_____

_____

_____

Challenge Yourself!

Think About It!

NAME: _____ **DATE:** _____

DIRECTIONS: Think about the problem. Answer the questions.

Tyler and Ally are playing an arcade game. Tyler wins 56 tickets. Ally wins 21 tickets. How many tickets do they win in all? Write two addition number sentences to solve the problem.

1. What do you know about the problem?

_____

_____

2. What do you need to find?

_____

_____

_____

3. How can you write two addition sentences to solve the problem?

_____

_____

_____

NAME: _____ **DATE:** _____

 DIRECTIONS: Read and solve the problem.

Problem: Tyler and Ally are playing an arcade game. Tyler wins 56 tickets. Ally wins 21 tickets. How many tickets do they win in all? Write two addition number sentences to solve the problem.

 **What Do You Know?**

 What Is Your Plan?

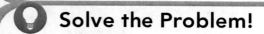 **Solve the Problem!**

 **Look Back and Explain!**

Picture It!

NAME: _____ **DATE:** _____

DIRECTIONS: Look at the example. Then, solve the problem by drawing base-ten blocks.

Example: Tyler and Ally play an arcade game. Ally wins 42 tickets. Tyler wins 25 tickets. How many tickets do they win in all?

42 + 25 = ☐   25 + 42 = ☐

$$40 + 20 = 60$$
$$2 + 5 = 7$$
$$60 + 7 = 67$$

$$20 + 40 = 60$$
$$5 + 2 = 7$$
$$60 + 7 = 67$$

Tyler and Ally play the game again. This time Tyler wins 52 tickets and Ally wins 46 tickets. How many tickets do they win in all?

52 + 46 = ☐   46 + 52 = ☐

_____   _____

_____   _____

_____   _____

NAME: _____ **DATE:** _____

 DIRECTIONS: Show two ways to solve the problem.

1. Tyler plays an arcade game three times. He wins 53 tickets on his first try, 12 tickets on his second try, and 34 tickets on his third try. How many tickets does he win in all?

Strategy 1 ·

Strategy 2 ·

2. How are the two strategies different? How are they the same?

_____

_____

_____

Solve It Two Ways!

Challenge Yourself!

NAME: _____ DATE: _____

Read and solve the problems.

1. Use the numbers in the squares to write an addition sentence. Use the numbers only once.

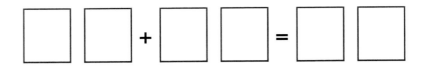

2. Write a different number sentence from the same fact family.

3. Write two subtraction sentences in the same fact family.

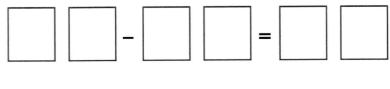

NAME: _____ DATE: _____

 DIRECTIONS: Think about the problem. Answer the questions.

The students in Ms. Jackson's class are having a jump-a-thon. Holly jumps 23 times. Kelly jumps 31 times. Leslie jumps 15 times. Anita jumps 20 times. How many times did all four girls jump?

1. What do you know about the problem?

_____

_____

2. What do you need to find?

_____

_____

_____

3. How can you solve the problem?

_____

_____

_____

Solve It!

NAME: _____ **DATE:** _____

DIRECTIONS: Read and solve the problem.

Problem: The students in Ms. Jackson's class are having a jump-a-thon. Holly jumps 23 times. Kelly jumps 31 times. Leslie jumps 15 times. Anita jumps 20 times. How many times did all four girls jump?

? **What Do You Know?**

🔑 **What Is Your Plan?**

💡 **Solve the Problem!**

🔍 **Look Back and Explain!**

NAME: _____ **DATE:** _____

 DIRECTIONS: Look at the example. Then, solve the problem.

Example: Mr. Bernard's students are jumping rope. David jumps 24 times. Miguel jumps 23 times. Duane jumps 31 times. How many times do the boys jump in all?

Tens	Ones	Number
▭▭	□ □ □ □	24
▭▭	□ □ □	23
▭▭▭	□	31
Total jumps		78

Mr. Bernard counts the number of jumps for the girls. Jada jumps 23 times. Lin jumps 22 times. Martina jumps 24 times. How many times do the girls jump in all?

Tens	Ones	Number
Total jumps		

Solve It Two Ways!

NAME: _____ DATE: _____

DIRECTIONS: Show two ways to solve the problem.

1. Ms. Stockton's students have a beanbag toss contest. On the first day, Michelle and Marcy each toss 24 beanbags. On the second day, Michelle and Marcy each toss 20 beanbags. How many beanbags do the girls toss in all?

· · · · Strategy 1 ·

· · · · Strategy 2 ·

2. How are the strategies different? How are they the same?

_____

_____

_____

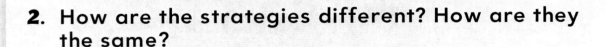

NAME: _____ **DATE:** _____

 DIRECTIONS: Read and solve the problem.

In a hula hoop contest, four students twirl their hula hoops 89 times. Use the numbers below to write an addition sentence to show the number of times they twirl the hula hoops. You may use the numbers more than once.

$$\boxed{0}\ \boxed{1}\ \boxed{2}\ \boxed{3}\ \boxed{4}$$
$$\boxed{5}\ \boxed{6}\ \boxed{7}\ \boxed{8}\ \boxed{9}$$

Challenge Yourself!

1. What number sentence can you write?

$$\square\square + \square\square + \square\square + \square\square = 89$$

2. Write a story problem about the number of times four students twirl their hula hoops.

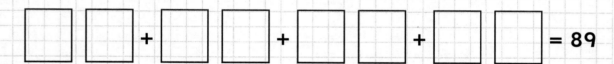

_____

_____

_____

_____

_____

NAME: _____ **DATE:** _____

Think About It!

DIRECTIONS: Think about the problem. Answer the questions.

There are two seals at the aquarium. One seal weighs 343 kilograms. The other seal weighs 356 kilograms. How many kilograms do the seals weigh altogether?

1. What do you know about the problem?

_____

_____

2. What do you need to find?

_____

_____

_____

3. How can you solve the problem?

_____

_____

_____

NAME: _____ DATE: _____

 DIRECTIONS: Read and solve the problem.

Solve It!

Problem: There are two seals at the aquarium. One seal weighs 343 kilograms. The other seal weighs 356 kilograms. How many kilograms do the seals weigh altogether? Use base-ten blocks to find your answer.

 **What Do You Know?**

 What Is Your Plan?

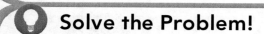 **Solve the Problem!**

 **Look Back and Explain!**

Picture It!

NAME: _____ DATE: _____

DIRECTIONS: Look at the example. Then, solve the problem using base-ten blocks.

Example: A stingray at the Seaside Aquarium weighs 321 kilograms. Another stingray weighs 264 kilograms. How many kilograms do the stingrays weigh altogether?

Hundreds	Tens	Ones	Number
		□	321
		□ □ □ □	264
Total kilograms			585

A sea turtle at the aquarium weighs 253 kilograms. Another sea turtle weighs 143 kilograms. How many kilograms do the sea turtles weigh altogether?

Hundreds	Tens	Ones	Number
Total kilograms			

NAME: _____ **DATE:** _____

 DIRECTIONS: Show two ways to solve the problem.

1. A young penguin is 35 centimeters tall. An adult penguin is 102 centimeters taller. How tall is the adult penguin?

Strategy 1

Draw base-ten blocks to solve the problem.

Strategy 2

Use a different strategy to solve the problem.

2. Which strategy do you like better? Explain your reasoning.

_____

_____

_____

Challenge Yourself!

NAME: _____ DATE: _____

DIRECTIONS: Read and solve the problem.

The smallest dolphin at an aquarium weighs a little more than 100 pounds. The largest dolphin weighs between 300 to 440 pounds.

1. Use the numbers in the squares to show how much the smallest dolphin could weigh. Use each number only once.

2. Use the numbers in the squares to show how much the largest dolphin could weigh. Use each number only once. Do not use the same numbers you used in problem 1.

NAME: _____ DATE: _____

 DIRECTIONS: Think about the problem. Answer the questions.

Mr. Hudson's class is playing a numbers game. Erik is thinking of a number that has 5 hundreds, 7 tens, and 2 ones. Sheila is thinking of a number that is 3 hundreds and 4 tens less than Erik's number. What number is Sheila thinking of?

1. What do you know about the problem?

_____

_____

2. What do you need to find?

_____

_____

_____

3. How can you solve the problem?

_____

_____

_____

NAME: _____ **DATE:** _____

Solve It!

 **DIRECTIONS:** Read and solve the problem.

Problem: Mr. Hudson's class is playing a numbers game. Erik is thinking of a number that has 5 hundreds, 7 tens, and 2 ones. Sheila is thinking of a number that is 3 hundreds and 4 tens less than Erik's number. What number is Sheila thinking of?

? **What Do You Know?**

🔑 **What Is Your Plan?**

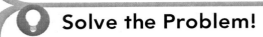 💡 **Solve the Problem!**

 🔍 **Look Back and Explain!**

#51614—180 Days of Problem Solving

NAME: _____ **DATE:** _____

 DIRECTIONS: Look at the example. Then, solve the problem.

Example: Find the sum of the addition problem. Write and solve a subtraction problem to check your answer.

Addition	Subtraction
780 + 219 999	999 − 219 780

Find the sum of the addition problem. Write and solve a subtraction problem to check your answer.

Addition	Subtraction
157 + 510	

Solve It Two Ways!

NAME: _____ DATE: _____

DIRECTIONS: Show two ways to solve the problem.

1. Bailey wants to find the sum of 345 and 531.

Strategy 1 ·

Write an addition problem to find the sum.

Strategy 2 ·

Write a subtraction problem to check your solution.

2. How did subtraction help you check your solution?

_____

_____

_____

NAME: _____ **DATE:** _____

 DIRECTIONS: Read and solve the problems.

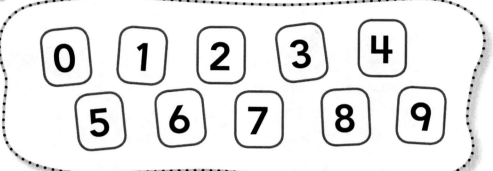

Challenge Yourself!

1. Use the numbers in the squares to write an addition sentence that equals 981. Use the numbers only once.

$$\square\ \square\ \square\ +\ \square\ \square\ \square\ = 981$$

2. Write a different number sentence from the same fact family.

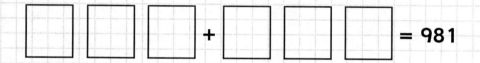

$$\square\ \square\ \square\ +\ \square\ \square\ \square\ = 981$$

3. Write two subtraction sentences from the same fact family.

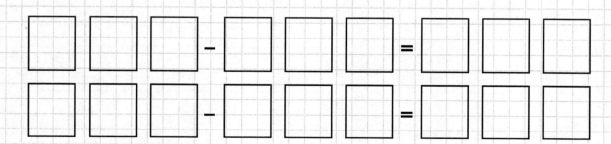

NAME: _____ **DATE:** _____

DIRECTIONS: Think about the problem. Answer the questions.

Think About It!

The top speed of an elephant is about 65 kilometers per hour. The top speed of a brown bear is about 10 kilometers per hour slower than the top speed of the elephant. What is the top speed of the brown bear?

1. **What do you know about the problem?**

   _____

   _____

2. **What do you need to find?**

   _____

   _____

   _____

3. **How can you solve the problem?**

   _____

   _____

   _____

#51614—180 Days of Problem Solving   © Shell Education

NAME: _____ **DATE:** _____

DIRECTIONS: Read and solve the problem.

Solve It!

Problem: The top speed of an elephant is about 65 kilometers per hour. The top speed of a brown bear is about 10 kilometers per hour slower than the top speed of the elephant. What is the top speed of the brown bear?

? What Do You Know?

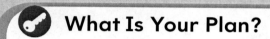
What Is Your Plan?

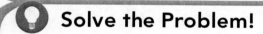
Solve the Problem!

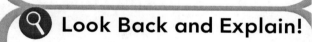
Look Back and Explain!

Picture It!

NAME: _____ **DATE:** _____

DIRECTIONS: Look at the example. Then, solve the problem using a number line.

Example: Gazelles can run up to 70 kilometers per hour. Elks run about 10 kilometers per hour slower than gazelles. How fast can an elk run?

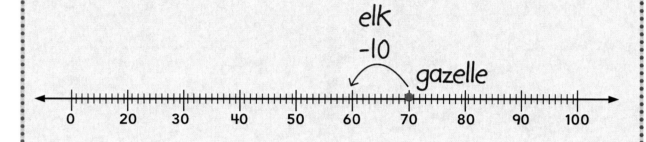

_____60_____ kilometers per hour

Giraffes can run up to 50 kilometers per hour. Hyenas run 10 kilometers per hour faster than giraffes. How fast can a hyena run?

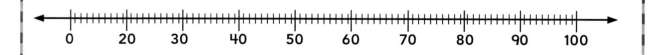

_____ kilometers per hour

NAME: _____ DATE: _____

 DIRECTIONS: Show two ways to solve the problem.

1. Polar bears can run up to 30 kilometers per hour. Squirrels run about 10 kilometers per hour slower than polar bears. Cheetahs run about 100 kilometers per hour faster than squirrels. How fast can a cheetah run?

Strategy 1 ···

Use the number line to solve the problem.

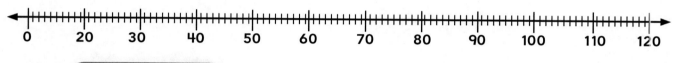

Strategy 2 ···

Use a different strategy to solve the problem.

2. Which strategy do you like better? Explain your reasoning.

_____

_____

_____

Challenge Yourself!

NAME: _____ **DATE:** _____

DIRECTIONS: Read and solve the problem.

Eagles can fly about 250 kilometers per hour. Falcons can fly about 100 kilometers per hour faster than eagles. Doves can fly about 100 kilometers per hour slower than eagles. Geese can fly about 10 kilometers per hour slower than doves.

1. What is the top speed of a falcon?

2. What is the top speed of a dove?

3. What is the top speed of a goose?

NAME: _____ **DATE:** _____

 DIRECTIONS: Think about the problem. Answer the questions.

Two seals weigh 698 kilograms. The weight of one of the seals is 358 kilograms. What is the weight of the other seal?

1. What do you know about the problem?

_____

_____

2. What do you need to find?

_____

_____

_____

3. How can you solve the problem?

_____

_____

_____

NAME: _____ **DATE:** _____

DIRECTIONS: Read and solve the problem.

Solve It!

Problem: Two seals weigh 698 kilograms. The weight of one of the seals is 358 kilograms. What is the weight of the other seal?

? **What Do You Know?**

What Is Your Plan?

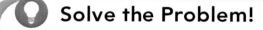 **Solve the Problem!**

 **Look Back and Explain!**

NAME: _____ DATE: _____

 DIRECTIONS: Look at the example. Then, solve the problem using base-ten blocks.

Example: Two ostriches weigh 265 kilograms. The weight of one ostrich is 132 kilograms. What is the weight of the other ostrich?

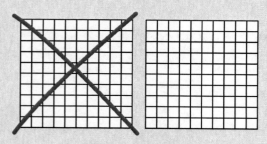 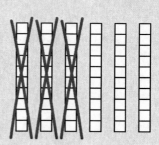

_____133_____ kilograms

Two tigers weigh 286 kilograms. The weight of one tiger is 154 kilograms. What is the weight of the other tiger?

_____ kilograms

Solve It Two Ways!

NAME: _____ DATE: _____

DIRECTIONS: Show two ways to solve the problem.

1. Two buffalo weigh 859 kilograms. The weight of one of the buffalo is 423 kilograms. How much does the other buffalo weigh?

Strategy 1

Draw base-ten blocks to solve the problem.

Strategy 2

Use a different strategy to solve the problem.

2. Which strategy do you think is easier? Explain your reasoning.

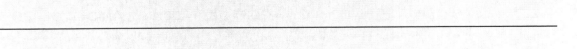

_____

_____

_____

NAME: _____ DATE: _____

 DIRECTIONS: Read and solve the problems.

1. Use the numbers in the squares to write an addition sentence. Use the numbers only once. Draw base-ten blocks to show how you found the sum.

2. Write a subtraction sentence in the same fact family. Use each number only once. Draw base-ten blocks to show how you found the difference.

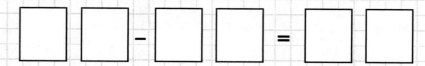

Think About It!

NAME: _____ **DATE:** _____

DIRECTIONS: Think about the problem. Answer the questions.

> Ms. Carter's class is measuring objects in their classroom. Which tool should they use to measure the height of the door? Use the tool to measure the height of the door in your room.

1. What do you know about the problem?

_____

_____

2. What do you need to find?

_____

_____

_____

3. How can you solve the problem?

_____

_____

_____

#51614—180 Days of Problem Solving

NAME: _____ **DATE:** _____

 DIRECTIONS: Read and solve the problem.

Problem: Ms. Carter's class is measuring objects in their classroom. Which tool should they use to measure the height of the door? Use the tool to measure the height of the door in your room.

 Solve It!

 **What Do You Know?**

What Is Your Plan?

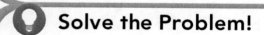 **Solve the Problem!**

 **Look Back and Explain!**

Picture It!

NAME: _____ **DATE:** _____

DIRECTIONS: Look at the example. Then, solve the problem.

Example: Use a ruler to measure the length of each fish in inches.

___2___ inches

___3___ inches

___4___ inches

Use a ruler to measure the length of each snake in centimeters.

_____ centimeters

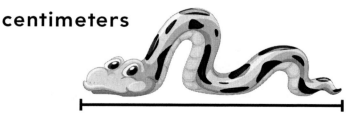

_____ centimeters   _____ centimeters

NAME: _____ DATE: _____

DIRECTIONS: Show two ways to solve the problem.

1. Measure your height and a friend's height. How tall are you? How tall is your friend?

Strategy 1

Measure with a yardstick or meterstick.

Strategy 2

Measure with a ruler.

2. Which strategy do you think is easier? Explain your reasoning.

_____

_____

_____

Challenge Yourself!

NAME: _____ DATE: _____

DIRECTIONS: Read and solve the problems.

1. Which tool can you use to measure the length of your pencil? Use the tool to measure.

   I measured a pencil with a _____.

   It is _____ long.

2. Which tool can you use to measure the length of your finger? Use the tool to measure.

   I measured my finger with a _____.

   It is _____ long.

3. Which tool can you use to measure the length of your shoe? Use the tool to measure.

   I measured my shoe with a _____.

   It is _____ long.

4. Choose an object to measure to the nearest foot. Use a tool to measure.

   I measured a _____ with a

   _____.

   It is _____ long.

NAME: _____ DATE: _____

DIRECTIONS: Think about the problem. Answer the questions.

Measure the length of the rectangle to the nearest inch. Then, measure the length to the nearest centimeter. Is the number of inches or the number of centimeters greater? Why?

length

1. **What do you know about the problem?**

_____

_____

2. **What do you need to find?**

_____

_____

_____

3. **How can you solve the problem?**

_____

_____

_____

Solve It!

NAME: _____ **DATE:** _____

DIRECTIONS: Read and solve the problem.

Problem: Measure the length of the rectangle to the nearest inch. Then, measure the length to the nearest centimeter. Is the number of inches or the number of centimeters greater? Why?

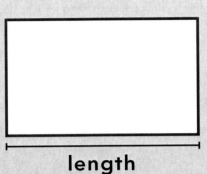

length

? **What Do You Know?**

What Is Your Plan?

Solve the Problem!

Check Your Work!

#51614—180 Days of Problem Solving

NAME: _____ **DATE:** _____

DIRECTIONS: Look at the example. Then, solve the problem.

Picture It!

Example: Measure the length of the sea creature to the nearest centimeter and to the nearest inch. Why are the measurements different?

_____3_____ centimeters _____l_____ inch

There are more __centimeters__ than __inches__

because a centimeter is ___smaller___.

Measure the length of the sea creature to the nearest centimeter and to the nearest inch. Why are the measurements different?

_____ centimeters _____ inches

There are fewer _____ than

_____ because an inch is _____.

#51614—180 Days of Problem Solving

Solve It Two Ways!

NAME: _____ DATE: _____

DIRECTIONS: Show two ways to solve the problem.

1. Measure the length of your desktop using two different tools. What is the length of your desktop to the nearest centimeter? What is the length of your desktop to the nearest foot?

> **Strategy 1** ···

Use a ruler to measure the length to the nearest centimeter.

_____ centimeters

> **Strategy 2** ···

Use a yardstick to measure the length to the nearest foot.

_____ feet

2. How are the sizes of the units different?

_____

_____

_____

NAME: _____ **DATE:** _____

DIRECTIONS: Read and solve the problems.

1. The length of Anita's bedroom is about 12 feet. The length of her bedroom is about 4 yards. Describe why the number of feet is different from the number of yards.

_____

_____

_____

_____

_____

2. The length of Anita's bed is 2 meters. The width is 1 meter. Will the length in centimeters be greater than, less than, or equal to the length in meters? How do you know?

_____

_____

_____

_____

Challenge Yourself!

Think About It!

NAME: _____ **DATE:** _____

DIRECTIONS: Think about the problem. Answer the questions.

The first string is 1 inch long. Estimate the length of the second string to the nearest inch.

estimate

1 inch

1. **What do you know about the problem?**

_____

_____

2. **What do you need to find?**

_____

_____

_____

3. **How can you solve the problem?**

_____

_____

_____

NAME: _____ **DATE:** _____

 DIRECTIONS: Read and solve the problem.

Problem: The first string is 1 inch long. Estimate the length of the second string to the nearest inch.

1 inch

? What Do You Know?

🔑 What Is Your Plan?

💡 Solve the Problem!

🔍 Look Back and Explain!

Picture It!

NAME: _____ **DATE:** _____

DIRECTIONS: Look at the example. Then, solve the problem.

Example: Find 3 objects to measure. Estimate the length of each object to the nearest centimeter. Then, use a ruler to measure the length of each object to the nearest centimeter.

├─┤
1 centimeter

Object	Estimated length (centimeters)	Actual length (centimeters)
pencil	12	15
stapler	17	16
scissors	20	20

Find 3 objects to measure. Estimate the length of each object to the nearest inch. Then, use a ruler to measure the length of each object to the nearest inch.

├────┤
1 inch

Object	Estimated length (inches)	Actual length (inches)

NAME: _____ **DATE:** _____

DIRECTIONS: Show two ways to solve the problem.

1. Find a big object to measure. Estimate the length of the object. Then, use a tool to measure the length.

Measurement 1

Estimate the length to the nearest foot.

_____ feet

Measure the length to the nearest foot.

_____ feet

Measurement 2

Estimate the length to the nearest meter.

_____ meters

Measure the length to the nearest meter.

_____ meters

2. How are the two measurements different?

_____

_____

_____

Challenge Yourself!

NAME: _____ DATE: _____

DIRECTIONS: Read and solve the problem.

Estimate and measure the length of one side of your room using different units.

1. **Estimate the length of the room to the nearest inch.**

   _____ inches

   Measure the length of the room to the nearest inch.

   _____ inches

2. **Estimate the length of the room to the nearest foot.**

   _____ feet

   Measure the length of the room to the nearest foot.

   _____ feet

3. **Estimate the length of the room to the nearest centimeter.**

   _____ centimeters

   Measure the length of the room to the nearest centimeter.

   _____ centimeters

4. **Estimate the length of the room to the nearest meter.**

   _____ meters

   Measure the length of the room to the nearest meter.

   _____ meters

NAME: _____ **DATE:** _____

DIRECTIONS: Think about the problem. Answer the questions.

Use a ruler to measure the length of each string to the nearest inch. What is the difference of the lengths?

String A

String B

1. **What do you know about the problem?**

   _____

   _____

2. **What do you need to find?**

   _____

   _____

   _____

3. **How can you solve the problem?**

   _____

   _____

   _____

NAME: _____ **DATE:** _____

DIRECTIONS: Read and solve the problem.

Solve It!

Problem: Use a ruler to measure the length of each string to the nearest inch. What is the difference of the lengths?

String A   String B

? What Do You Know?

🔑 What Is Your Plan?

💡 Solve the Problem!

🔍 Look Back and Explain!

NAME: _____ **DATE:** _____

 DIRECTIONS: Look at the example. Then, solve the problem.

Example: Use the ruler to measure the length of each car to the nearest centimeter. What is the difference?

Car A	Car B

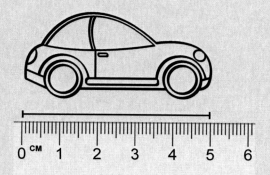 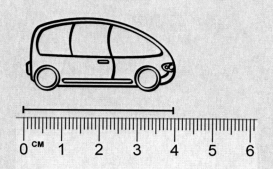

5 centimeters   _4 centimeters_

5 – 4 = 1 centimeter

Use the ruler to measure the length of each truck to the nearest centimeter. What is the difference?

Truck A   Truck B

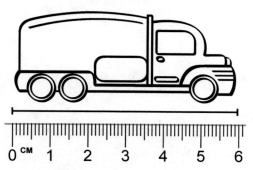 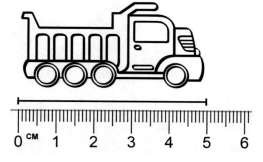

_____   _____

_____

Solve It Two Ways!

NAME: _____ DATE: _____

DIRECTIONS: Show two ways to solve the problem.

1. Measure the length of your room to the nearest yard. Measure the width of your room to the nearest yard. What is the difference between the length and the width?

Strategy 1

Use a ruler to measure.

Strategy 2

Use a yardstick to measure.

2. Which strategy do you think is better? Explain your reasoning.

_____

_____

_____

NAME: _____ **DATE:** _____

DIRECTIONS: Read and solve the problem.

Work with a friend. Find out who can hop farther.

1. Mark a starting point and stand behind the line. Hop as far as you can. Mark where you landed. What is the distance between the two points, to the nearest centimeter?

   _____ centimeters

2. Have your friend stand behind the line. Tell your friend to hop as far as possible. Mark where your friend lands. What is the distance between the two points to the nearest centimeter?

   _____ centimeters

3. Who hopped farther? What is the difference between the two lengths?

   _____

   _____

   _____

   _____

   _____

Think About It!

NAME: _____ **DATE:** _____

DIRECTIONS: Think about the problem. Answer the questions.

The world record for the longest paper airplane flight is about 76 yards. The old record was about 65 yards. What is the difference between the two distances?

1. What do you know about the problem?

_____

_____

2. What do you need to find?

_____

_____

_____

3. How can you solve the problem?

_____

_____

_____

NAME: _____ **DATE:** _____

 DIRECTIONS: Read and solve the problem.

Problem: The world record for the longest paper airplane flight is about 76 yards. The old record was about 65 yards. What is the difference between the two distances?

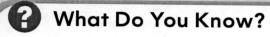 **What Do You Know?**

 What Is Your Plan?

 **Solve the Problem!**

 **Look Back and Explain!**

Picture It!

NAME: _____ DATE: _____

DIRECTIONS: Look at the example. Then, solve the problem using a number line.

Example: Vince throws a baseball 36 yards. Jamal throws the baseball 23 yards farther than Vince. How far does Jamal throw the baseball?

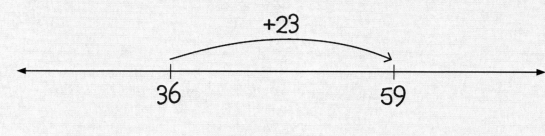

36 + 23 = 59 yards

Stephanie throws the baseball 24 yards. Alexis throws the baseball 15 yards farther than Stephanie. How far does Alexis throw the baseball?

NAME: _____ **DATE:** _____

DIRECTIONS: Show two ways to solve the problem.

1. Hannah built a fence that is 22 meters long. Juanita also built a fence. The total length of the two fences is 53 meters. How long is the fence that Juanita built?

   Strategy 1

   Write an addition sentence to solve the problem.

   Strategy 2

   Write a subtraction sentence to solve the problem.

2. Which strategy do you think is easier? Explain your reasoning.

   _____

   _____

   _____

NAME: _____ **DATE:** _____

DIRECTIONS: Read and solve the problem.

Tammy and Heidi each have a ribbon. The difference between the lengths is 12 centimeters. The length of Tammy's ribbon is 34 centimeters.

Challenge Yourself!

1. What could be the length of Heidi's ribbon? Write an addition sentence to show how to find the length.

   _____

   _____ centimeters

2. What could be another length for Heidi's ribbon? Write a subtraction sentence to show how to find the length.

   _____

   _____ centimeters

3. Explain why there could be two different solutions for this problem.

   _____

   _____

   _____

   _____

   _____

#51614—180 Days of Problem Solving
© *Shell Education*

NAME: _____ DATE: _____

 DIRECTIONS: Think about the problem. Answer the questions.

A ham sandwich is 14 inches long. A tuna sandwich is 11 inches long. How many inches of sandwich are there in all?

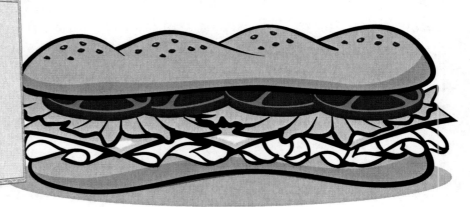

1. What do you know about the problem?

_____

_____

2. What do you need to find?

_____

_____

_____

3. How can you solve the problem?

_____

_____

_____

Solve It!

NAME: _____ **DATE:** _____

DIRECTIONS: Read and solve the problem.

Problem: A ham sandwich is 14 inches long. A tuna sandwich is 11 inches long. How many inches of sandwich are there in all? Use the number line to solve the problem.

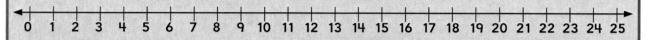
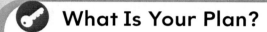

? What Do You Know?

🔑 What Is Your Plan?

💡 Solve the Problem!

🔍 Look Back and Explain!

NAME: _____ DATE: _____

 **DIRECTIONS:** Look at the example. Then, solve the problem using a number line.

Example: Sam's pencil is 13 centimeters long. Kelly's pencil is 12 centimeters long. How long are the pencils end to end?

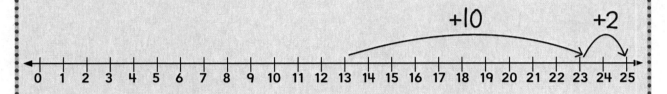

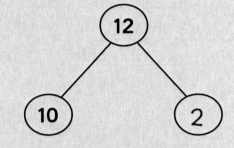

$$\begin{array}{r} 13 \\ +\ 10 \\ \hline 23 \end{array} \qquad \begin{array}{r} 23 \\ +\ 2 \\ \hline 25 \end{array}$$

Sam's piece of yarn is 11 centimeters long. Kelly's piece of yarn is 13 centimeters long. How long are the pieces of yarn end to end?

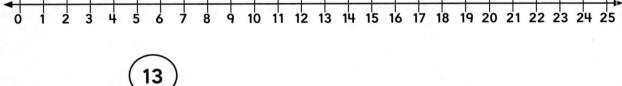

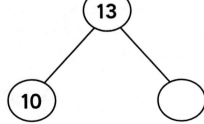

Solve It Two Ways!

NAME: _____ DATE: _____

DIRECTIONS: Show two ways to solve the problem.

1. Juan has a string that is 80 centimeters long. He cuts a piece that is 15 centimeters long to use for an art project. How many centimeters of string does Juan have left?

Strategy 1

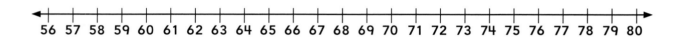

56 57 58 59 60 61 62 63 64 65 66 67 68 69 70 71 72 73 74 75 76 77 78 79 80

Strategy 2

Use a different strategy to solve the problem.

2. Which strategy do you think is easier? Explain your reasoning.

_____

_____

_____

NAME: _____ DATE: _____

 DIRECTIONS: Read and solve the problem.

Nika is using a number line to figure out how many minutes she watched a movie.

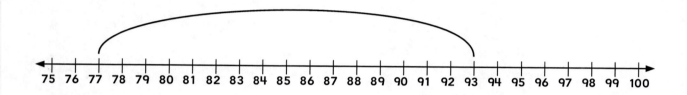

75 76 77 78 79 80 81 82 83 84 85 86 87 88 89 90 91 92 93 94 95 96 97 98 99 100

1. Write an addition sentence that can be solved using this number line. Explain your thinking.

2. Write a subtraction sentence that can be solved using this number line. Explain your thinking.

Think About It!

NAME: _____ **DATE:** _____

DIRECTIONS: Think about the problem. Answer the questions.

This clock shows the time Beatrice wakes up in the morning. What time does she wake up?

1. **What do you know about the problem?**

_____

_____

2. **What do you need to find?**

_____

_____

_____

3. **How can you solve the problem?**

_____

_____

_____

NAME: _____ **DATE:** _____

 DIRECTIONS: Read and solve the problem.

Problem: This clock shows the time Beatrice wakes up in the morning. What time does she wake up? Use a.m. or p.m. in your answer.

Solve It!

 What Do You Know?

What Is Your Plan?

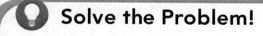 **Solve the Problem!**

 **Look Back and Explain!**

Picture It!

NAME: _____ **DATE:** _____

DIRECTIONS: Look at the example. Then, solve the problem.

Example: This clock shows the time Reggie starts school. What time does he start school? Use a.m. or p.m. in your answer.

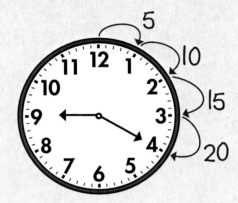

___9___ : ___20___ ___a.m.___

This clock shows the time Reggie finishes school. What time does he finish school? Use a.m. or p.m. in your answer.

_____ : _____ _____

NAME: _____ DATE: _____

 DIRECTIONS: Show two ways to solve the problem.

1. Jorge's birthday party will start at two forty-five. What does two forty-five look like on a clock?

Strategy 1

Show the time on the digital clock.

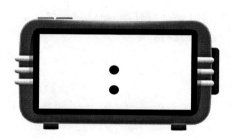

Strategy 2

Show the time on the analog clock.

2. Which strategy do you like better? Explain your reasoning.

_____

_____

_____

NAME: _____ DATE: _____

DIRECTIONS: Read and solve the problem.

Sophia starts her math homework at 3:55 p.m. She finishes her math homework in 30 minutes.

1. Show the time Sophia starts her homework on the analog clock.

2. Show the time Sophia finishes her homework on the digital clock.

3. Use words, numbers, or pictures to show how you found the time Sophia finishes her homework.

NAME: _____ **DATE:** _____

DIRECTIONS: Think about the problem. Answer the questions.

> Keiko has 2 quarters and 7 pennies in her piggy bank. How much money does she have?

1. **What do you know about the problem?**

_____

_____

2. **What do you need to find?**

_____

_____

_____

3. **How can you solve the problem?**

_____

_____

_____

Solve It!

NAME: _____ **DATE:** _____

DIRECTIONS: Read and solve the problem.

Problem: Keiko has 2 quarters and 7 pennies in her piggy bank. How much money does she have?

? What Do You Know?

🔑 What Is Your Plan?

💡 Solve the Problem!

🔍 Look Back and Explain!

#51614—180 Days of Problem Solving

NAME: _____ **DATE:** _____

 Look at the example. Then, solve the problem.

Example: Koi earns money for doing chores. How much money does he earn?

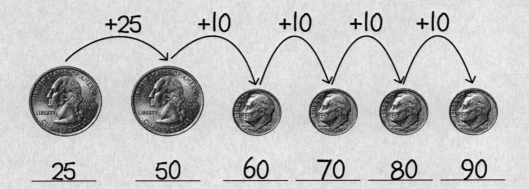

+25 +10 +10 +10 +10

__25__ __50__ __60__ __70__ __80__ __90__

Koi earns ____90____ cents.

Colleen earns money for doing chores. How much money does she earn?

___ ___ ___ ___ ___ ___ ___ ___ ___

Colleen earns _____ cents.

NAME: _____ **DATE:** _____

Solve It Two Ways!

DIRECTIONS: Show two ways to solve the problem.

1. Marisol has 72 cents in her pocket. What coins might she have?

Strategy 1 ·

Strategy 2 ·

2. How are the two strategies different? How are they the same?

_____

_____

_____

NAME: _____ **DATE:** _____

DIRECTIONS: Read and solve the problem.

Caitlin, Mickey, and Kimberly have money to spend at a snack shack. Caitlin has the most money. Mickey has more money than Kimberly.

1. Complete the table to show the number of dollars and coins each person might have.

	Dollar	Quarter	Dime	Nickel	Penny	Total
Caitlin						
Mickey						
Kimberly						

2. Use the information from the table to write a story problem about the money each person has.

_____

_____

_____

_____

_____

_____

_____

Challenge Yourself!

Think About It!

DIRECTIONS: Think about the problem. Answer the questions.

Mr. Jackson's class measures their bean plants to see how much they grew. They make a line plot to show the data.

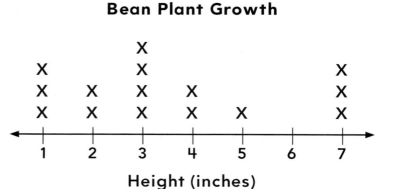

Bean Plant Growth

Height (inches)

1. **What do you know about the problem?**

_____

_____

2. **Write a question that can be answered from the line plot.**

_____

_____

3. **How tall are the shortest bean plants? How tall are the tallest bean plants? How do you know?**

_____

_____

_____

NAME: _____ DATE: _____

 DIRECTIONS: Read and solve the problem.

Solve It!

Problem: Mr. Jackson's class measures their bean plants to see how much they grew. They make a line plot to show the data. How many bean plants are 3 inches tall?

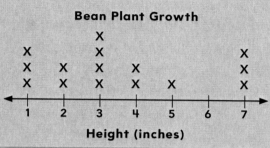

Bean Plant Growth

Height (inches)

 **What Do You Know?**

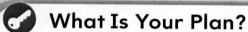 **What Is Your Plan?**

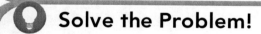 **Solve the Problem!**

 **Look Back and Explain!**

Picture It!

NAME: _____ **DATE:** _____

DIRECTIONS: Look at the example. Then, solve the problem.

Example: Salma measures the flowers in her garden. Create a line plot to show the heights of the flowers.

Flower	Height (centimeters)
1	8
2	14
3	7
4	9
5	10
6	5
7	10
8	12
9	10
10	8

Flower Growth

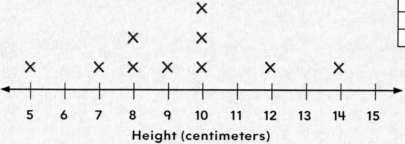

Height (centimeters)

Denzel measures the tomato plants in his garden. Create a line plot to show the heights of the tomato plants.

Plant	Height (centimeters)
1	20
2	15
3	16
4	20
5	14
6	14
7	18
8	16
9	20
10	15

Tomato Plant Growth

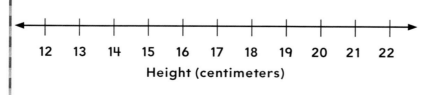

Height (centimeters)

NAME: _____ **DATE:** _____

DIRECTIONS: Show two ways to solve the problem.

1. George measures the length, in inches, of 10 toy airplanes. He makes a list of the lengths in this order: 9, 6, 7, 5, 3, 6, 2, 4, 5, 7.

Strategy 1

Show the data in a table.

Toy Airplane	Length (inches)
1	
2	
3	
4	
5	
6	
7	
8	
9	
10	

Strategy 2

Show the data on a line plot.

Toy Airplane Length

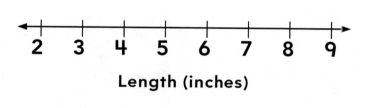

Length (inches)

2. Which strategy do you like better? Explain your reasoning.

_____

_____

_____

Challenge Yourself!

NAME: _____ DATE: _____

DIRECTIONS: Read and solve the problem.

Measure the lengths of five different shoes to the nearest inch.

1. Record the measurements of the shoes in the table.

Shoe	Length (inches)
1	
2	
3	
4	
5	

2. Write the measurements from shortest to longest.

_____

3. Create a line plot to show the measurements.

Title: _____

_____

NAME: _____ DATE: _____

DIRECTIONS: Think about the problem. Answer the questions.

This bar graph shows the number of meters four kids ran at school.

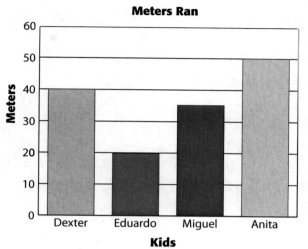

1. **What do you know about the problem?**

   _____

   _____

2. **How can you find the number of meters each kid ran?**

   _____

   _____

   _____

3. **Write a question that can be answered from the bar graph.**

   _____

   _____

Solve It!

NAME: _____ **DATE:** _____

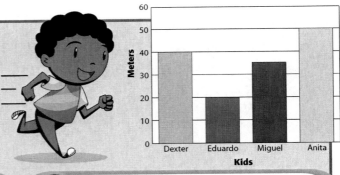

DIRECTIONS: Read and solve the problem.

Problem: The bar graph shows the number of meters four kids ran at school. How many more meters did Miguel run than Eduardo?

? What Do You Know?

🔑 What Is Your Plan?

💡 Solve the Problem!

🔍 Look Back and Explain!

NAME: _____ **DATE:** _____

 DIRECTIONS: Look at the example. Then, solve the problem.

Example: Carlos is on a hockey team. The table shows the number of goals his team scored during the first four games. Complete the bar graph to show this data.

Game	Goals
1	3
2	0
3	5
4	2

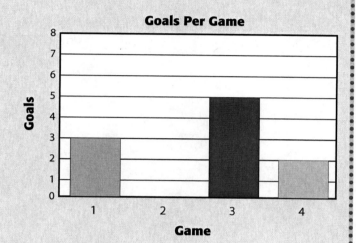

Serena is on a soccer team. The table shows the number of goals her team scored during the first four soccer games. Complete the bar graph to show this data.

Goals Per Game

Game	Goals
1	2
2	5
3	4
4	1

Solve It Two Ways!

NAME: _____ DATE: _____

DIRECTIONS: Show two ways to solve the problem.

1. Bree is on a basketball team. She recorded the number of baskets she made in the first 4 games in this order: 8, 5, 4, 6.

Strategy 1

Show the data using a table.

Game	Baskets
1	
2	
3	
4	

Strategy 2

Show the data using a bar graph.

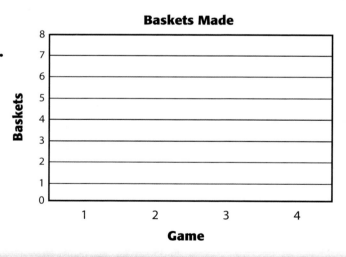

Baskets Made

2. Which strategy do you think is better? Explain your reasoning.

_____

_____

_____

NAME: _____ **DATE:** _____

DIRECTIONS: Read and solve the problem.

Laura and her friends were playing football. Use the information below to find the number of yards each girl threw the football.

- Laura threw the football 3 yards.

- Maria threw the football 2 yards more than Laura.

- Sarah threw the football 3 yards less than Maria.

- Jean threw the football the same number of yards Laura and Sarah threw the football combined.

1. Show the number of yards each girl threw the football in the table.

Girl	Yards
Laura	
Maria	
Sarah	
Jean	

2. Make a bar graph to show the data.

Title: _____

```
8 |_____
7 |_____
6 |_____
5 |_____
4 |_____
3 |_____
2 |_____
1 |_____
0 |_____
```

_____ _____ _____ _____ _____

_____

NAME: _____ **DATE:** _____

Think About It!

DIRECTIONS: Think about the problem. Answer the questions.

> I have 3 sides and 3 angles. What am I?

1. What do you know about the problem?

_____

_____

2. What do you need to do to solve the problem?

_____

_____

_____

3. Can a shape with 3 sides have 4 angles? Explain your thinking.

_____

_____

_____

NAME: _____ **DATE:** _____

 DIRECTIONS: Read and solve the problem.

Problem: I have 3 sides and 3 angles. What am I?

❓ What Do You Know?

🔑 What Is Your Plan?

💡 Solve the Problem!

🔍 Look Back and Explain!

Picture It!

NAME: _____ **DATE:** _____

DIRECTIONS: Look at the example. Then, solve the problem.

Example: Draw a circle around each triangle. Draw an X on each quadrilateral. What is the name of the shape you did not mark?

_____ pentagon _____

Draw a circle around each triangle. Draw an X on each quadrilateral. What is the name of the shape you did not mark?

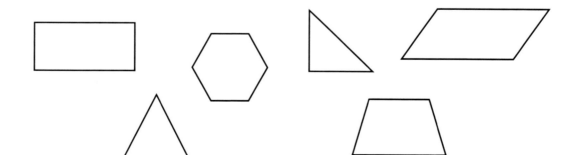

_____

#51614—180 Days of Problem Solving

NAME: _____ **DATE:** _____

DIRECTIONS: Show two ways to solve the problem.

1. Jamila wants to draw two pictures using a triangle, a quadrilateral, and a pentagon.

Picture 1

Draw a picture with a triangle, a quadrilateral, and a pentagon.

Picture 2

Draw another picture with a different type of triangle, quadrilateral, and pentagon.

2. How are the two pictures the same? How are they different?

_____

_____

_____

NAME: _____ DATE: _____

DIRECTIONS: Read and solve the problem.

Sergio wants to draw a picture of a quadrilateral and a triangle. How can Sergio draw these shapes?

Describe how the number of sides, angles, and faces are different between the shapes you drew.

_____

_____

_____

_____

_____

NAME: _____ **DATE:** _____

DIRECTIONS: Think about the problem. Answer the questions.

How can you partition a rectangle into 8 squares that are all the same size? How many rows will there be? How many squares will be in each row?

1. **What do you know about the problem?**

_____

_____

2. **What do you need to find?**

_____

_____

3. **How can you solve the problem?**

_____

_____

_____

Solve It!

NAME: _____ DATE: _____

DIRECTIONS: Read and solve the problem.

Problem: How can you partition a rectangle into 8 squares that are all the same size? How many rows will there be? How many squares will be in each row?

? What Do You Know?

🔑 What Is Your Plan?

💡 Solve the Problem!

🔍 Look Back and Explain!

NAME: _____ **DATE:** _____

DIRECTIONS: Look at the example. Then, solve the problem.

Example: Partition the rectangle into 3 rows and 4 columns. How many equal parts did you make?

column
↓

←row

___12___ equal parts

Partition the rectangle into 5 rows and 3 columns. How many equal parts did you make?

_____ equal parts

Solve It Two Ways!

NAME: _____ DATE: _____

DIRECTIONS: Show two ways to solve the problem.

1. Show two ways you can partition a rectangle into 6 equal squares. How many rows are there? How many squares are in each row? Draw a picture for each solution.

Solution 1

_____ rows

_____ squares in each row

Solution 2

_____ rows

_____ squares in each row

2. How are the two solutions different? How are they the same?

_____

_____

_____

© Shell Education

NAME: _____ **DATE:** _____

 DIRECTIONS: Read and solve the problem.

Ronald partitioned the rectangle to show a number.

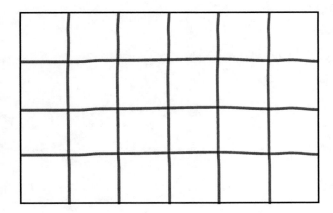

1. What number did Ronald show? _____

2. Is there another way to show the number? Draw another solution.

Think About It!

NAME: _____ **DATE:** _____

DIRECTIONS: Think about the problem. Answer the questions.

Partition the circle into two equal parts. What word describes the equal parts?

1. **What do you know about the problem?**

   _____

   _____

2. **What do you need to find?**

   _____

   _____

   _____

3. **How can you solve the problem?**

   _____

   _____

   _____

NAME: _____ **DATE:** _____

 DIRECTIONS: Read and solve the problem.

Problem: Partition the circle into two equal parts. What word describes the equal parts?

? **What Do You Know?**

🔑 **What Is Your Plan?**

💡 **Solve the Problem!**

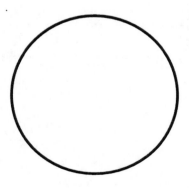

_____

🔍 **Look Back and Explain!**

Picture It!

NAME: _____ DATE: _____

DIRECTIONS: Look at the example. Then, solve the problems.

Example: Partition the circle into thirds. How many equal parts are there?

_____3_____ equal parts

1. Partition the square into halves. How many equal parts are there?

_____ equal parts

2. Partition the square into thirds. How many equal parts are there?

_____ equal parts

#51614—180 Days of Problem Solving   © Shell Education

NAME: _____ **DATE:** _____

DIRECTIONS: Show two ways to solve the problem.

1. Partition a rectangle into fourths two different ways. How many equal parts are there?

Strategy 1

_____ equal parts

Strategy 2

_____ equal parts

2. How are the two strategies the same? How are they different?

_____

_____

_____

Challenge Yourself!

NAME: _____ DATE: _____

 **DIRECTIONS:** Read and solve the problem.

Marissa has a paper triangle. She wants to partition it into smaller triangles. How can Marissa partition her triangle into equal parts?

1. Show three ways to partition the triangle into halves. How many halves does each triangle have?

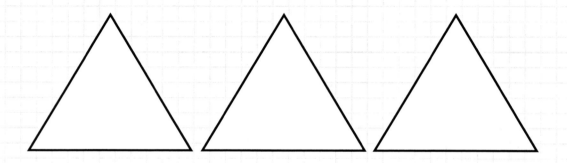

_____ halves

2. Show how to partition the triangle into thirds. How many thirds are there?

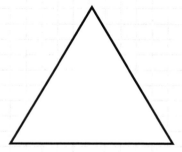

_____ thirds

3. Show how to partition the triangle into fourths. How many fourths are there?

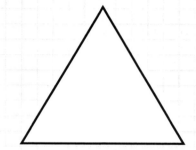

_____ fourths

ANSWER KEY

Week 1: Day 1 (page 13)
1. There are 10 craft sticks in each bundle. There are 300 craft sticks.
2. Find how many bundles of 10 are in 300 craft sticks.
3. Possible answer: I can draw pictures of bundles of 10 craft sticks and count the bundles by 10 until I reach the number 300.

Week 1: Day 2 (page 14)
30 bundles; there are 10 craft sticks in each bundle and a total of 300 craft sticks; find how many bundles of 10 are in 300 craft sticks; draw a picture of bundles of 10 craft sticks and count the bundles by 10 until reach the number 300

Week 1: Day 3 (page 15)

Number	Hundreds	Tens	Ones
365			

Week 1: Day 4 (page 16)
1. Strategy 1: 23 tens blocks and 6 ones blocks

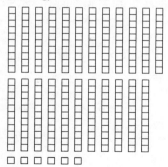

Strategy 2: 2 hundreds blocks, 3 tens blocks, and 6 units

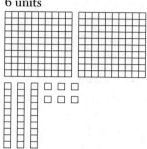

2. Possible answer: In Strategy 1, there are 23 tens and 6 ones. In Strategy 2, there are 2 hundreds, 3 tens, and 6 ones. In Strategy 2, 10 tens are grouped to make 1 hundred.

Week 1: Day 5 (page 17)
1. Possible answer: 1 hundred block, 3 tens blocks, and 4 ones blocks
2. Possible answer: 1 hundred block and 34 ones blocks

Week 2: Day 1 (page 18)
1. Each bundle has 10 straws.
2. Find the number of straws.
3. Possible answer: I can count by 10s until I count all of the bundles.

Week 2: Day 2 (page 19)
120 straws; 10, 20, 30, 40, 50, 60, 70, 80, 90, 100, 110, 120; each bundle has 10 straws; find the number of straws by counting by tens

Week 2: Day 3 (page 20)

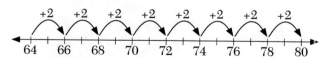

Week 2: Day 4 (page 21)
1. 35 flowers; Strategy 1: students should have written the numbers 1–35; Strategy 2: students should have written the numbers 5, 10, 15, 20, 25, 30, 35
2. Possible answer: I think counting by fives is easier because I can find my answer much faster than counting by ones.

ANSWER KEY *(cont.)*

Week 2: Day 5 (page 22)
1. Students should have completed the hundreds chart with the missing numbers: 5, 10, 18, 24, 30, 32, 35, 38, 44, 45, 46, 48, 50, 52, 53, 57, 59, 61, 63, 67, 68, 70, 75, 77, 78, 81, 83, 85, 86, 87, 88, 91, 92, 95, 98; students should have colored all the multiples of 10 in yellow; possible patterns are all the numbers end in zero and all the numbers are in the last column in the chart.
2. Students should have colored all the multiples of 5 in blue; possible patterns are all numbers end in 5 or 0 and all numbers are in the middle column or last column of the chart. The multiples of 10 are colored in both yellow and blue because the multiples of 10 are also the multiples of 5.

Week 3: Day 1 (page 23)
1. Juan's address is six hundred fifty-eight.
2. Find the numbers that show six hundred fifty-eight.
3. Possible answer: I will change the number from word form to number form by using base-ten blocks.

Week 3: Day 2 (page 24)
658; Juan's address is six hundred fifty-eight; find the numbers that show six hundred fifty-eight by using base-ten blocks

Week 3: Day 3 (page 25)
The picture shows 2 hundreds 6 tens 8 ones. The number is 268.

Week 3: Day 4 (page 26)
1. Strategy 1: 800 + 40 + 2; Strategy 2: 842
2. Possible answer: In Strategy 1, the values of each digit are being added together to show the number. In Strategy 2, the values of each digit were added together to show the number.

Week 3: Day 5 (page 27)
1. 300 + 20 + 8
2. three hundred twenty-eight
3. 328

Week 4: Day 1 (page 28)
1. The numbers being compared are 624 and 608.
2. Compare the numbers 624 and 608 using >, <, or =.
3. Possible answer: I can use base-ten blocks by showing the amount of hundreds, tens, and ones for each number. Then, I can compare the hundreds blocks for each number. If one number has more hundreds, then that number is greater. If the two numbers have the same number of hundreds, I will compare the tens blocks. If the two numbers have the same number of tens, I will compare the ones blocks.

Week 4: Day 2 (page 29)
624 > 608; the numbers being compared are 624 and 608; compare the numbers 624 and 608 using >, <, or =; use base-ten blocks to compare the number of hundreds, tens, and ones in each number; 624 and 608 have the same number of hundreds; 624 has more tens than 608

Week 4: Day 3 (page 30)
207 is less; 230 > 207; student should have drawn base-ten blocks to represent each number

Week 4: Day 4 (page 31)
1. 245 pounds; Strategy 1: student should have drawn base-ten blocks to show each number and circled 245; Strategy 2: 200 + 10 + 5 = 215; 200 + 40 + 5 = 245; 245 > 215 or 215 < 245
2. Possible answer: I think drawing base-ten blocks to show each number is better because it helps me compare the number of hundreds, tens, and ones. The number with more hundreds is greater. If they have the same number of hundreds, I can compare the number of tens. Since 245 has more tens than 215, it is greater.

Week 4: Day 5 (page 32)
1. Possible answer: 945 > 867
2. Possible answer: 125 < 142
3. Possible answer: 349 = 349
4. Possible answer: I used base-ten blocks to compare the numbers. I wrote a number and used hundreds blocks to help me find a number that is greater than, less than, or equal to that number.

ANSWER KEY (cont.)

Week 5: Day 1 (page 33)
1. One cow weighs 732 pounds and another cow weighs 832 pounds.
2. Find the cow that weighs more.
3. 732 = 7 hundreds, 3 tens, and 2 ones
   832 = 8 hundreds, 3 tens, and 2 ones

Week 5: Day 2 (page 34)
832 > 732; one cow weighs 732 pounds and another cow weighs 832 pounds; draw a picture of base-ten blocks to show each number; use <, >, or = to compare the numbers

Week 5: Day 3 (page 35)
4 hundreds 6 tens 7 ones; 467 pounds

Week 5: Day 4 (page 36)
1. Accept two solutions that are greater than 225 but less than 250.
2. Possible answer: I know that both solutions must be greater than 225, but less than 250. I wrote the numbers 234 and 249. Both numbers have a greater number of tens than 225, but less tens than 250.

Week 5: Day 5 (page 37)
1. Possible answer: 406 > 257
2. Mr. Rodriquez has 406 acres on his farm. Mr. Gonzalez has 257 acres on his farm. Which farmer has a greater number of acres on his farm?

Week 6: Day 1 (page 38)
1. The numbers 9, 4, and 13 belong to a fact family.
2. Find two addition sentences and two subtraction sentences that use the numbers 9, 4, and 13.
3. Possible answer: I can write two addition sentences that have sum of 13. I can write one subtraction sentence with a difference of 9. I can write one subtraction sentence with a difference of 4.

Week 6: Day 2 (page 39)
9 + 4 = 13, 4 + 9 = 13, 13 − 4 = 9, 13 − 9 = 4; the numbers 9, 4, and 13 belong to a fact family; write two addition sentences that have sum of 13; write one subtraction sentence with a difference of 9; write one subtraction sentence with a difference of 4

Week 6: Day 3 (page 40)
13 toy trucks

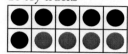
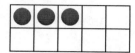

Week 6: Day 4 (page 41)
1. 8 stickers; Strategy 1: student should have colored in 13 circles in the ten frames and crossed out 5 of the circles; Strategy 2: student should have counted back 5 from 13: 13, 12, 11, 10, 9, 8
2. Possible answer: I think using ten frames is easier than counting back because after I take 5 away from 13 then I can count how many are left. Counting on is easier for me than counting back.

Week 6: Day 5 (page 42)

+	1	2	3	4	5	6	7	8	9	10
1	2	3	4	5	6	7	8	9	10	11
2	3	4	5	6	7	8	9	10	11	12
3	4	5	6	7	8	9	10	11	12	13
4	5	6	7	8	9	10	11	12	13	14
5	6	7	8	9	10	11	12	13	14	15
6	7	8	9	10	11	12	13	14	15	16
7	8	9	10	11	12	13	14	15	16	17
8	9	10	11	12	13	14	15	16	17	18
9	10	11	12	13	14	15	16	17	18	19
10	11	12	13	14	15	16	17	18	19	20

Possible answer: I can find one addend in the first column and the other addend in the top row. Where they meet in the table is the sum of the addition problem.

Week 7: Day 1 (page 43)
1. Jack has 13 blue blocks and 14 green blocks.
2. Find the number of blocks Jack has in all.
3. Student should have drawn base-ten blocks to show each number; Possible answer for 13: 1 tens block and 3 ones blocks; Possible answer for 14: 1 tens block and 4 ones blocks

ANSWER KEY *(cont.)*

Week 7: Day 2 (page 44)

27 blocks; Jack has 13 blue blocks and 14 green blocks; arrange the blocks into groups of tens and ones and add them together

Week 7: Day 3 (page 45)

12 + 7 = 19

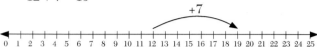

Week 7: Day 4 (page 46)

1. 38 crayons; Strategy 1: student should have colored in 26 circles in red and 12 circles in blue to show a total of 38; Strategy 2: student should have counted on 12 more from 26: 26, 27, 28, 29, 30, 31, 32, 33, 34, 35, 36, 37, 38

2. Possible answer: I think counting on is easier because if I start on 26 then I just count on 12 more. Counting on is faster than coloring in the ten frames and then counting them all up.

Week 7: Day 5 (page 47)

1. Possible answer: 12 + 35 = 47

2. Possible story problem: Anthony has 12 yellow markers and 35 red markers. How many markers does Anthony have in all?

Week 8: Day 1 (page 48)

1. Dominic and his mother make 25 cookies and then they make 23 more cookies.

2. Find the total number of cookies Dominic and his mother make.

3. Possible answer: I can add 25 and 23 to find the total number of cookies.

Week 8: Day 2 (page 49)

48 cookies; 25 + 23 = 48; Dominic and his mother make 25 cookies and then make 23 more cookies; add 25 and 23 to find the total number of cookies

Week 8: Day 3 (page 50)

17 children; 9 + 8 = 17

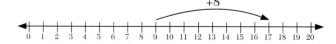

Week 8: Day 4 (page 51)

1. 29 party hats; Strategy 1: student should have counted on 11 more from 18: 18, 19, 20, 21, 22, 23, 24, 25, 26, 27, 28, 29; Strategy 2: student should have colored in 29 of the circles in the ten frames

2. Possible answer: I think counting on is easier. I started with 18 and counted on 11 more to get 29.

Week 8: Day 5 (page 52)

1. Possible answer: 35 + 21 = 56

2. Possible story problem: At Dominic's birthday party, the children play games for 35 minutes. Then, Dominic's mother reads a story to the children for 21 minutes. How many minutes did the children play games and listen to a story?

Week 9: Day 1 (page 53)

1. Olivia scores 89 points on the first video game she plays and scores 57 points on the second video game.

2. Find the difference between the points Olivia scores on the two video games.

3. Possible answer: I will write a subtraction sentence Olivia can use to find the difference between the points she scores on the video games.

Week 9: Day 2 (page 54)

32 points; 89 − 57 = 32; Olivia scores 89 points on the first video game she plays and scores 57 points on the second video game; write a subtraction sentence to find the difference between the points she scores on the video games.

Week 9: Day 3 (page 55)

41 points; 63 − 22 = 41

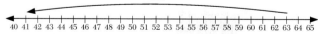

Week 9: Day 4 (page 56)

1. 22 points; Strategy 1: student should have used the number line by drawing an arrow from 43 to 21 to find the answer 22; Strategy 2: student should have counted back from 43 to 21 to find the answer 22

2. Possible answer: I think using a number line is easier because I can start on 43 and move 21 spaces backwards on the number line to get my answer, 22.

ANSWER KEY *(cont.)*

Week 9: Day 5 (page 57)
1. Possible answer: 98 – 46 = 52
2. Possible story problem: Jamie plays two video games. She scores a total of 98 points on both games. She scores 46 points on the second game. How many points does she score on the first game?

Week 10: Day 1 (page 58)
1. In Mr. Sullivan's library, there are 87 books and 23 of the books are books about dinosaurs.
2. Find how many books in the library are not about dinosaurs.
3. Student should have drawn base-ten blocks to show the number 87 and then crossed out 23 blocks to show the problem. Possible picture for 87: 8 tens blocks and 7 ones blocks. Student should have crossed out 2 tens blocks and 3 ones blocks.

Week 10: Day 2 (page 59)
64 books; 87 – 23 = 64; there are 87 books in the library and 23 of those books are about dinosaurs; draw a picture of 8 tens and 7 ones and cross out 2 tens and 3 ones

Week 10: Day 3 (page 60)
19 – 16 = 3

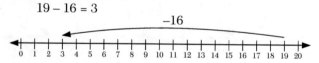

Week 10: Day 4 (page 61)
1. 11 books; Strategy 1: student should have colored in 19 circles and crossed out 8 in the ten frames to find the answer 11; Strategy 2: student should have counted back 8 from 19 to find the answer 11.
2. Possible answer: I think using ten frames is easier because I can color in 19 circles and then cross out 8 circles to find my answer, 11.

Week 10: Day 5 (page 62)
1. Possible answer: 59 – 16 = 43
2. Possible story problem: In Ms. Bing's library, there are 59 fiction books and 16 non-fiction books. What is the difference between the number of fiction books and the number of non-fiction books?

Week 11: Day 1 (page 63)
1. Emily sells 34 cupcakes on Monday, 42 cupcakes on Tuesday, and 21 cupcakes on Wednesday.
2. Find the total number of cupcakes Emily sells on the three days.
3. Possible answer: I can add 34 and 42 and then add 21 to find the total.

Week 11: Day 2 (page 64)
97 cupcakes; 34 + 42 = 76; 76 + 21 = 97; or 21 + 42 + 34 = 97; Emily sells 34 cupcakes on Monday, 42 cupcakes on Tuesday, and 21 cupcakes on Wednesday; add 34 and 42 and then add 21 to find the total

Week 11: Day 3 (page 65)
13 + 14 = 27; 27 + 10 = 37

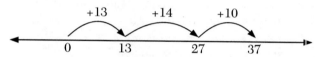

Week 11: Day 4 (page 66)
1. 59 eggs; Strategy 1: student should have used an open number line to solve the problem; Strategy 2: Student may have used equations, base-ten blocks, ten frames: 16 + 32 = 48; 48 + 11 = 59; or 16 + 32 + 11 = 59

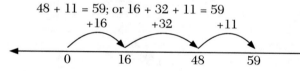

2. Possible answer: I think writing equations is easier because I can add two numbers by their place values and then add the third number to the sum.

Week 11: Day 5 (page 67)
1. Possible answer: 30 + 41 + 27 = 98
2. Student should have shown work to prove the sum is 98; Possible strategies; equations, base-ten blocks, ten frames: 30 + 41 = 71; 71 + 27 = 98

ANSWER KEY *(cont.)*

Week 12: Day 1 (page 68)
1. Karen's paper airplane flew a distance of 39 feet. Leslie's airplane flew a distance of 11 feet less than Karen's airplane. Cheryl's airplane flew a distance of 6 feet less than Leslie's airplane.
2. Find the distance Cheryl's airplane flew.
3. Possible answer: I can use subtraction to find the distance Karen's airplane flew and then use subtraction to find the distance Cheryl's airplane flew.

Week 12: Day 2 (page 69)
22 feet; 39 – 11 = 28, 28 – 6 = 22; Karen's paper airplane flew a distance of 39 feet; Leslie's airplane flew a distance of 11 feet less than Karen's airplane; Cheryl's airplane flew a distance of 6 feet less than Leslie's airplane; subtract 11 from 39 to find the distance Karen's airplane flew and then subtract 6 from my answer to find the distance Cheryl's airplane flew

Week 12: Day 3 (page 70)
23 inches; 46 – 13 = 33; 33 – 10 = 23

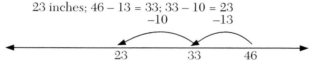

Week 12: Day 4 (page 71)
1. 31 inches; Strategy 1: student should have used an open number line to solve the problem; Strategy 2: student may have used equations, base-ten blocks, ten frames to solve the problem: 76 – 21 = 55; 55 – 24 = 31

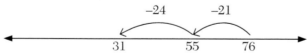

2. Possible answer: I like to use a number line better because it helps me understand what is happening in the story problem.

Week 12: Day 5 (page 72)
1. Possible answer: 49 – 12 – 25 = 12
2. Student should have shown work to prove the number sentence is true; Possible strategies; equations, base-ten blocks, or ten frames:
49 – 12 = 37; 37 – 25 = 12

Week 13: Day 1 (page 73)
1. A pig can run 11 miles per hour, a squirrel can run 9 miles per hour faster than a pig, and a mouse can run 12 miles per hour slower than a squirrel.
2. Find the speed a squirrel can run and the speed a mouse can run.
3. Possible answer: I can find the speed of the squirrel by adding 9 miles to the speed of the pig. I can find the speed of the mouse by subtracting 12 miles from the speed of the squirrel.

Week 13: Day 2 (page 74)
A squirrel can run 20 miles per hour; 11 + 9 = 20; a mouse can run 8 miles per hour; 20 – 12 = 8; a pig can run 11 miles per hour, a squirrel can run 9 miles per hour faster than a pig, a mouse can run 12 miles per hour slower than a squirrel; find the speed of the squirrel by adding 9 miles to the speed of the pig; find the speed of the mouse by subtracting 12 miles from the speed of the squirrel

Week 13: Day 3 (page 75)
70 – 40 = 30; 30 – 10 = 20

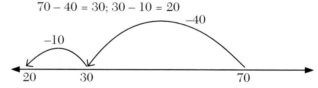

Week 13: Day 4 (page 76)
1. 47 miles per hour; Strategy 1: student should have used the open number line to solve the problem; Strategy 2; student may have used equations, base-ten blocks, or ten frames to solve the problem: 42 + 45 = 87; 87 – 40 = 47

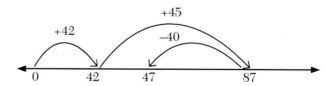

2. Possible answer: I think writing equations is easier because I can add the speed of the fox and elk together and then subtract the speed of the ostrich from my sum.

ANSWER KEY *(cont.)*

Week 13: Day 5 (page 77)
1. 54 – 12 = 42 miles per hour
2. 54 + 42 = 96 miles per hour
3. Student should have shown how they solved the problem; Possible strategies: number line; base-ten blocks; addition problem using place value

Week 14: Day 1 (page 78)
1. On Saturday, there were 55 visitors at City Zoo and on Sunday, there were 22 less visitors than on Saturday.
2. Find how many total visitors there were on Saturday and Sunday.
3. Possible answer: I need to find the number of visitors on Sunday by using subtraction. Then, I need to find the total number of visitors on Saturday and Sunday by using addition.

Week 14: Day 2 (page 79)
88 visitors; 55 – 22 = 33; 55 + 33 = 88; On Saturday, there were 55 visitors at City Zoo and on Sunday, there were 22 less visitors than on Saturday; subtract 22 from 55 to find the number of visitors on Saturday; add 55 and the difference to find the number of visitors on both Saturday and Sunday

Week 14: Day 3 (page 80)
49 – 16 = 33; 33 – 23 = 10; student should have crossed out 39 of the 49 shaded circles in the ten frames

Week 14: Day 4 (page 81)
1. There are the same number of students in the second-grade classrooms and in the third-grade classrooms; Strategy 1: student should have used the ten frames to solve the problem by either shading in 49 circles with one color and 49 more circles with another color to compare them or shading in 49 circles and then crossing out 49 circles; Strategy 2: student may have used a number line, base-ten blocks, or equations: 2 tens + 5 ones + 2 tens + 4 ones = 4 tens + 9 ones = 49 students in the second-grade classrooms; 2 tens + 3 ones + 2 tens + 6 ones = 4 tens + 9 ones = 49 students in the third-grade classrooms; 4 tens – 4 tens + 9 ones – 9 ones = 0
2. Possible answer: I think using base-ten blocks is easier because I can combine the tens blocks for each number and the ones blocks for each number and then compare to see how many more students there are.

Week 14: Day 5 (page 82)
1. Possible answer: 30 + 27 + 31 = 88
2. Student should have shown work to prove the number sentence is correct; Possible strategies: number line, base-ten blocks, equations, ten frames

Week 15: Day 1 (page 83)
1. There are 8 clowns and each clown is holding 2 balloons.
2. Find how many balloons there are.
3. Possible answer: I can count by twos to find the total number of balloons.

Week 15: Day 2 (page 84)
16 balloons; 2, 4, 6, 8, 10, 12, 14, 16; there are 8 clowns and each clown is holding 2 balloons; count by twos to find the total number of balloons

Week 15: Day 3 (page 85)
13; odd; There are 6 groups of 2 with 1 left over; students should have drawn circles around groups of 2 squares

Week 15: Day 4 (page 86)
1. Even number; Strategy 1: student should have drawn a picture to show 18 is an even number by make groups of 2; Strategy 2: student should have counted by twos and wrote the numbers 2, 4, 6, 8, 10, 12, 14, 16, 18
2. Possible answer: I think counting by twos is easier because I know if I count by twos and I say the number, then the number is even.

Week 15: Day 5 (page 87)
1. Possible answers: 6 + 6 = 12 or 10 + 2 = 12 or 4 + 8 = 12; 2 + 2 = 4; 4 + 4 = 8 or 2 + 6 = 8

Number	20	17
2. Is the number even or odd?	even	odd
3. Use words, numbers, pictures to show your thinking.	Possible answer: 10 + 10 = 20	Possible answer:

ANSWER KEY *(cont.)*

Week 16: Day 1 (page 88)
1. There are 3 rows and 5 stickers in each row.
2. Find how many stickers Damien has.
3. Possible answer: I can add the number of stickers in each row.

Week 16: Day 2 (page 89)
   15 pictures; 5 + 5 + 5 = 15; there are 3 rows and 5 pictures in each row; add the number of pictures in each in each row

Week 16: Day 3 (page 90)
   5 + 5 = 10; There are 10 cookies. Student should have made 2 circles around each row of 5 cookies.

Week 16: Day 4 (page 91)
1. 6 rainbows; Strategy 1: 3 + 3 = 6; Strategy 2: 2 + 2 + 2 = 6
2. Possible answer: The first strategy has 2 equal groups of 3 and the second strategy has 3 equal groups of 2. Both strategies have a sum of 6.

Week 16: Day 5 (page 92)
   Student should have drawn 4 different arrays with a total of 12. Possible arrays and addition sentences: 4 rows of 3, 3 + 3 + 3 + 3 = 12; 3 rows of 4, 4 + 4 + 4 = 12; 2 rows of 6, 6 + 6 = 12; 6 rows of 2, 2 + 2 + 2 + 2 + 2 + 2 = 12; 1 row of 12, 12 + 0 = 12; 12 rows of 1, 1 + 1 + 1 + 1 + 1 + 1 + 1 + 1 + 1 + 1 + 1 + 1 = 12

Week 17: Day 1 (page 93)
1. There are 5 rows and 5 desks in each row.
2. Find the number of desks.
3. Possible answer: I can add the number of desks in each row.

Week 17: Day 2 (page 94)
   25 desks; 5 + 5 + 5 + 5 + 5 = 25; there are 5 rows and 5 desks in each row; find the number of desks by drawing an array; add the number of desks in each row

Week 17: Day 3 (page 95)
   Possible arrays and addition sentences: 2 rows of 5, 5 + 5 = 10; 5 rows of 2, 2 + 2 + 2 + 2 + 2 = 10; 1 row of 10, 10 + 0 = 10; 10 rows of 1, 1 + 1 + 1 + 1 + 1 + 1 + 1 + 1 + 1 + 1 = 10

Week 17: Day 4 (page 96)
1. Possible arrays and addition sentences: 3 rows of 5, 5 + 5 + 5 = 15; 5 rows of 3, 3 + 3 + 3 + 3 + 3 = 15
2. Possible answer: For the first strategy, I made an array with 3 rows of 5. For the second strategy, I wrote the addition sentence 5 + 5 + 5 = 15. Both strategies show there are 3 rows with 5 in each row.

Week 17: Day 5 (page 97)
1. Student should have drawn 4 different arrays with a total of 24. Possible arrays and addition sentences: 2 rows of 12, 12 + 12 = 24; 12 rows of 2, 2 + 2 + 2 + 2 + 2 + 2 + 2 + 2 + 2 + 2 + 2 + 2 = 24; 3 rows of 8, 8 + 8 + 8 = 24; 8 rows of 3, 3 + 3 + 3 + 3 + 3 + 3 + 3 + 3 = 24; 4 rows of 6, 6 + 6 + 6 + 6 = 24; 6 rows of 4, 4 + 4 + 4 + 4 + 4 + 4 = 24; 1 row of 24, 24 + 0 = 24; 24 rows of 1, 1 + 1 + 1 + 1 + 1 + 1 + 1 + 1 + 1 + 1 + 1 + 1 + 1 + 1 + 1 + 1 + 1 + 1 + 1 + 1 + 1 + 1 + 1 + 1 = 24

Week 18: Day 1 (page 98)
1. Two addition sentences have 56 and 21 as the addends.
2. Find the sum of each of the addition sentences.
3. Possible answer: I know that when I switch the order of the addends, I will still get the same sum. So, I can write two addition sentences with the same addends by switching the addends.

Week 18: Day 2 (page 99)
   56 + 21 = 77 and 21 + 56 = 77; two addition sentences have 56 and 21 as the addends; write two addition sentences and find the sum

Week 18: Day 3 (page 100)
   52 + 46 = 98; 50 + 40 = 90; 2 + 6 = 8; 90 + 8 = 98; 46 + 52 = 98; 40 + 50 = 90; 6 + 2 = 8; 90 + 8 = 98; Student should have drawn base-ten blocks to represent each number

ANSWER KEY *(cont.)*

Week 18: Day 4 (page 101)
1. 53 + 12 + 34 = 99; Possible strategies: student may have added the first two numbers and then added the third number to the sum (53 + 12 = 65; 65 + 34 = 99); or added the last two numbers and then added the first number to the sum (12 + 34 = 46; 46 + 53 = 99)
2. Possible answer: For the first strategy, I added the first two numbers and then I added the last number to my sum. For the second strategy, I added the last two numbers and then I added the first number. Both strategies have a sum of 99.

Week 18: Day 5 (page 102)
1. Possible answer: 13 + 46 = 59
2. Possible answer: 46 + 13 = 59
3. Possible answer: 59 − 46 = 13 and 59 − 13 = 46

Week 19: Day 1 (page 103)
1. Holly jumps 23 times, Kelly jumps 31 times, Leslie jumps 15 times, and Anita jumps 20 times.
2. Find how many times the four girls jumped
3. Possible answer: I can add the four numbers to find the total.

Week 19: Day 2 (page 104)
89 jumps; 23 + 31 + 15 + 20 = 89; Holly jumps 23 times, Kelly jumps 31 times, Leslie jumps 15 times, and Anita jumps 20 times; add the four numbers to find the total number of jumps the four girls did; possible strategies: number line, base-ten blocks, equations, ten frames

Week 19: Day 3 (page 105)

Tens	Ones	Number
▭▭	□ □ □	23
▭▭	□ □	22
▭▭	□ □ □ □	24
	Total jumps:	69

Week 19: Day 4 (page 106)
1. 88 beanbags; Possible strategies: student may have doubled 24 and doubled 20 and then added them together [(24 + 24) + (20 + 20) = 48 + 40 = 88]; or student my have doubled 20 and doubled 24 and added them together [(20 + 20) + (24 + 24) = 40 + 48 = 88]
2. Possible answer: For the first strategy, I added 24 and 24. Then, I added 20 and 20. Lastly, I added the two sums together to find the total number of beanbags. For the second strategy, I added 20 and 20. Then, I added 24 and 24. Lastly, I added the two sums together to find the total number of beanbags. Both strategies have a sum of 88.

Week 19: Day 5 (page 107)
1. Possible answer: 20 + 21 + 22 + 26 = 89
2. Possible story problem: William, Henry, Mindy, and Tonya spin a hula hoop. William spins the hula hoop 20 times. Henry spins the hula hoop 21 times. Mindy spins the hula hoop 22 times. Tonya spins the hula hoop 26 times. How many spins did they make in all?

Week 20: Day 1 (page 108)
1. One seal weighs 343 kilograms, and another seal weighs 356 kilograms.
2. Find the total number of kilograms both seals weigh.
3. Possible answer: I can use base-ten blocks to show the number of hundreds, tens, and ones in each number. Then, I can add the number of hundreds, tens, and ones to find the total.

Week 20: Day 2 (page 109)
699 kilograms; 343 + 356 = 699; one seal weighs 343 kilograms and another seal weighs 356 kilograms; use base-ten blocks to show the number of hundreds, tens, and ones in each number; add the number of hundreds, tens, and ones to find the total

ANSWER KEY *(cont.)*

Week 20: Day 3 (page 110)

Hundreds	Tens	Ones	Number
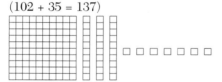			253
			143
		Total kilograms:	396

Week 20: Day 4 (page 111)

1. 137 centimeters; Strategy 1: student should have drawn base-ten blocks to solve the problem; Strategy 2: student may have used a number line, ten frames, or equations
    (102 + 35 = 137)

2. Possible answer: I like using base-ten blocks to add numbers. I can use hundreds, tens, and ones blocks to build each number, and then I can add them together to find the total.

Week 20: Day 5 (page 112)

1. Possible answer: 102
2. Possible answer: 347

Week 21: Day 1 (page 113)

1. Erik is thinking of a number that has 5 hundreds, 7 tens, and 2 ones. Sheila is thinking of a number that is 3 hundreds and 4 tens less than the number Erik is thinking of.
2. Find the number Sheila is thinking of.
3. Possible answer: I can take 3 hundreds from 5 hundreds and 4 tens from 7 tens to find Sheila's number.

Week 21: Day 2 (page 114)

232; 5 hundreds – 3 hundreds = 2 hundreds; 7 tens – 4 tens = 3 tens; 2 hundreds + 3 tens + 2 ones = 232; Erik is thinking of a number that has 5 hundreds, 7 tens, and 2 ones; Sheila is thinking of a number that is 3 hundreds and 4 tens less than the number Erik is thinking of; subtract 3 hundreds from 5 hundreds; subtract 4 tens from 7 tens

Week 21: Day 3 (page 115)

Addition	Subtraction	
157 + 510 667	667 – 157 510 or	667 – 510 157

Week 21: Day 4 (page 116)

1. Strategy 1: 345 + 531 = 876;
    Strategy 2: 876 – 345 = 531 or 876 – 531 = 345
2. I subtracted 345 from 876 and got the answer 531. The numbers are from the same fact family.

Week 21: Day 5 (page 117)

1. Possible answer: 420 + 561 = 981
2. Possible answer: 561 + 420 = 981
3. Possible answer: 981 – 561 = 420 and 981 – 420 = 561

Week 22: Day 1 (page 118)

1. The top speed of an elephant is about 65 kilometers per hour. The top speed of a brown bear is about 10 kilometers less than the top speed of an elephant.
2. Find the top speed of the brown bear.
3. Possible answer: I can subtract 10 from 65 to find the top speed of the brown bear.

Week 22: Day 2 (page 119)

55 kilometers per hour; 65 – 10 = 55; top speed of an elephant is about 65 kilometers per hour; top speed of a brown bear is about 10 kilometers per hour less than the top speed of an elephant; subtract 10 from 65

Week 22: Day 3 (page 120)

60 kilometers per hour

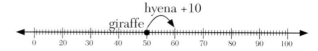

ANSWER KEY *(cont.)*

Week 22: Day 4 (page 121)
1. 120 kilometers per hour; Strategy 1: student should have used a number line to solve the problem; Strategy 2: student may have used base-ten blocks, ten frames, or equations to solve the problem (30 – 10 = 20; 20 + 100 = 120)

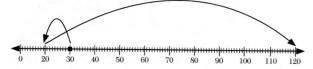

2. Possible answer: I like using a number line because I can move backwards on the number line to subtract numbers and forward to add numbers.

Week 22: Day 5 (page 122)
1. 350 kilometers per hour; 250 + 100 = 350
2. 150 kilometers per hour; 250 – 100 = 150
3. 140 kilometers per hour; 150 – 10 = 140

Week 23: Day 1 (page 123)
1. The combined weight of two seals is 698 kilograms. The weight of one of the seals is 358 kilograms.
2. Find the weight of the other seal.
3. Possible answer: I can use base-ten blocks to subtract the weight of one of the seals (358) from the combined weight (698).

Week 23: Day 2 (page 124)
340 kilograms; 698 – 358 = 340; combined weight of two seals is 698 kilograms; weight of one of the seals is 358 kilograms; subtract 358 from 698

Week 23: Day 3 (page 125)
132 kilograms; student should have drawn 2 hundreds blocks, 8 tens blocks, and 6 ones blocks, and crossed out 1 hundreds block, 5 tens blocks, and 4 ones blocks.

Week 23: Day 4 (page 126)
1. 436 kilograms: Strategy 1: Student should have drawn 8 hundreds blocks, 5 tens blocks, and 9 ones blocks, and crossed out 4 hundreds blocks, 2 tens blocks, and 3 ones blocks; Strategy 2: 859 – 423 = ☐; 859 – 423 = 436
2. Possible answer: Using base-ten blocks is easier for me. I started with 8 hundreds blocks, 5 tens blocks, and 9 ones blocks to show 859. Then, I took away 4 hundreds blocks, 2 tens blocks, and 3 ones blocks to subtract 423. I had 4 hundreds blocks, 3 tens blocks, and 6 ones blocks left. My answer is 436.

Week 23: Day 5 (page 127)
1. Possible answer: 25 + 43 = 68; student should have drawn base-ten blocks to show the sum
2. Possible answer: 68 – 25 = 43; student should have drawn base-ten blocks to show the difference

Week 24: Day 1 (page 128)
1. Use a tool to measure the height of the door in the room.
2. Find a tool to measure the height of the door in the room.
3. Possible answer: I will use a measuring tape to measure the door in my room. (A ruler or yardstick are also possible answers.)

Week 24: Day 2 (page 129)
Possible answer: 90 inches; use a tool to measure the height of the door in the room; a measuring tape to measure the height of the door (ruler or yardstick are also possible answers)

Week 24: Day 3 (page 130)
10; 5; 7

Week 24: Day 4 (page 131)
1. Accept any reasonable measurements of the heights; Possible answer: 54 inches; Strategy 1: student should have used a yardstick to measure his or her height; Strategy 2: student should have used a ruler to measure a friend's height
2. Possible answer: I think using a yardstick is easier because when I used the ruler it was hard to keep track of where to place it when I had to keep stacking it.

ANSWER KEY *(cont.)*

Week 24: Day 5 (page 132)
1. Possible answer: I measured a pencil with a ruler. It is 12 centimeters long.
2. Possible answer: I measured my finger with a ruler. It is 5 centimeters long.
3. Possible answer: I measured my shoe with a measuring tape. It is 6 inches long.
4. Possible answer: I measured a car with a yardstick. It is 6 feet long.

Week 25: Day 1 (page 133)
1. Measure the length of the rectangle using an inch ruler and a centimeter ruler.
2. Find the length of the rectangle to the nearest inch and to the nearest centimeter.
3. Possible answer: I can use a ruler to find the length to the nearest inch and to the nearest centimeter.

Week 25: Day 2 (page 134)
Length: 2 inches; 5 centimeters; the number of centimeters is greater because a centimeter is a smaller unit than an inch; measure the length of the rectangle using an inch ruler and a centimeter ruler

Week 25: Day 3 (page 135)
5 centimeters; 2 inches; There are fewer inches than centimeters because an inch is bigger.

Week 25: Day 4 (page 136)
1. Accept any reasonable measurement of the length of the desktop; Strategy 1: student should have used a ruler to measure the length to the nearest centimeter; Possible answer: 60 centimeters; Strategy 2: student should have used a yardstick to measure the length to the nearest foot; Possible answer: 2 feet
2. Possible answer: A centimeter is a smaller unit than a foot, so the number for centimeters is much greater than the number for feet.

Week 25: Day 5 (page 137)
1. The number for the amount of feet is greater than the number for yards because a foot is a smaller unit than a yard.
2. The number of centimeters will be greater than the number for meters because a centimeter is a smaller unit than a meter.

Week 26: Day 1 (page 138)
1. The length of the first string is 1 inch.
2. Estimate the length of the second string.
3. Possible answer: I can use the length of the first string to estimate the length of the second string.

Week 26: Day 2 (page 139)
About 3 inches; the length of the first string is 1 inch; estimate the length of the second string by using the length of the first string

Week 26: Day 3 (page 140)
Accept any reasonable estimates for the lengths of three objects to the nearest inch.

Week 26: Day 4 (page 141)
1. Accept any reasonable estimates for the length of a big object. Strategy 1: student should have estimated and then measured the length of the big object to the nearest foot; Strategy 2: student should have estimated and then measured the length of the big object to the nearest meter
2. Possible answer: The number for the amount of feet was greater than the number for the amount of meters because a foot is smaller than a meter.

Week 26: Day 5 (page 142)
1. Accept any reasonable estimate and actual measurement of the length of the room to the nearest inch: Possible answer for estimate: 500 inches: Possible answer for actual measurement: 396 inches
2. Accept any reasonable estimate and actual measurement of the length of the room to the nearest foot; Possible answer for estimate: 30 feet; Possible answer for actual measurement: 33 feet
3. Accept any reasonable estimate and actual measurement of the length of the room to the nearest centimeter; Possible answer for estimate: 1,200 centimeters; Possible answer for actual measurement: 1,000 centimeters
4. Accept any reasonable estimate and actual measurement of the length of the room to the nearest meter; Possible answer for estimate: 12 meters; Possible answer for actual measurement: 10 meters

ANSWER KEY *(cont.)*

Week 27: Day 1 (page 143)
1. There are two strings to measure the length to the nearest inch.
2. Find the difference between the length of the two strings.
3. Possible answer: I can use an inch ruler to find the measurements of the two strings. Then, I can use subtraction to find the difference between the two measurements.

Week 27: Day 2 (page 144)
String A: 2 inches; String B: 4 inches; 4 – 2 = 2 inches; there are two strings to measure the length to the nearest inch; use an inch ruler to find the measurements of the two strings; use subtraction to find the difference between the two measurements

Week 27: Day 3 (page 145)
Truck A: 6 centimeters; Truck B: 5 centimeters; 6 – 5 = 1 centimeter

Week 27: Day 4 (page 146)
1. Accept any reasonable measurement of the length and width of the room; Accept any reasonable answer for the difference between the length and width to the nearest yard; Strategy 1: student should have used a ruler to measure the length and width to the nearest yard; Strategy 2: student should have used a yardstick to measure the length and width to the nearest yard; Possible answer for length: 5 yards; Possible answer for width: 4 yards; 5 – 4 = 1 yard
2. Possible answer: I think using a yardstick to measure the length and width of the room is better than using a ruler. I didn't have to move the yardstick as many times as I did when using the ruler.

Week 27: Day 5 (page 147)
1. Accept any reasonable measurement for the length of a hop to the nearest centimeter; Possible answer: 60 centimeters
2. Accept any reasonable measurement for the length of a hop to the nearest centimeter; Possible answer: 50 centimeters
3. Accept any reasonable difference between the two hops: Possible answer: 60 – 50 = 10 centimeters

Week 28: Day 1 (page 148)
1. The longest indoor distance a paper airplane flew is approximately 76 yards. A previous indoor distance a paper airplane flew is approximately 65 yards.
2. Find the difference between the two distances.
3. Possible answer: I need to write a subtraction sentence to show how to find the difference and then solve the problem.

Week 28: Day 2 (page 149)
11 yards; 76 – 65 = 11; the longest indoor distance a paper airplane flew is about 76 yards; a previous indoor distance a paper airplane flew is about 65 yards; write a subtraction sentence to show how to find the difference and then solve the problem

Week 28: Day 3 (page 150)
24 + 15 = 39 yards

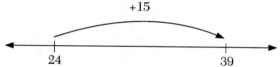

Week 28: Day 4 (page 151)
1. 31 meters; Strategy 1: □ + 22 = 53; 31 + 22 = 53; Strategy 2: 53 – 22 = □; 53 – 22 = 31
2. Possible answer: I think writing a subtraction sentence to solve the problem is easier because I can subtract the numbers by their place values. I can subtract 3 ones minus 2 ones, which is 1 one. Then, I can subtract 5 tens minus 2 tens, which is 3 tens. My answer is 3 tens and 1 one, or 31.

Week 28: Day 5 (page 152)
1. 34 + 12 = 46; 46 centimeters
2. 34 – 12 = 22; 22 centimeters
3. Possible answer: There could be two solutions to the story problem because it does not tell whether Tammy's ribbon is the shorter ribbon or the longer ribbon.

Week 29: Day 1 (page 153)
1. A ham sandwich is 14 inches long. A tuna sandwich is 11 inches long.
2. The number of inches long for both sandwiches.
3. Possible answer: I can add 14 and 11 by using the number line.

ANSWER KEY *(cont.)*

Week 29: Day 2 (page 154)

25 inches; 14 + 11 = 25; a ham sandwich is 14 inches; a tuna sandwich is 11 inches; add 14 and 11 using the number line

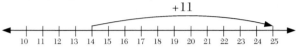

Week 29: Day 3 (page 155)

11 + 10 = 21; 21 + 3 = 24

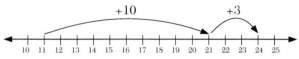

Week 29: Day 4 (page 156)

1. 65 centimeters; 80 − 15 = 65; Strategy 1: student should have used the number line to solve the problem; Strategy 2: student may have used base-ten blocks, ten frames, or a subtraction problem
2. Possible answer: I think using base-ten blocks is easier because I can start with 8 tens and then take away 1 ten and 5 ones. I have 6 tens and 5 ones left, so my answer is 65.

Week 29: Day 5 (page 157)

1. Possible answers: 77 + 16 = 93; 77 + 10 + 6 = 93; 77 + 3 + 10 + 3 = 93
2. Possible answers: 93 − 16 = 77; 93 − 3 − 13 = 77; 93 − 3 − 10 − 3 = 77

Week 30: Day 1 (page 158)

1. The clock shows the time Beatrice woke up in the morning.
2. Find the time Beatrice woke up in the morning.
3. Possible answer: I need to look at the hour hand to find the number of hours and the minute hand to find the number of minutes that the clock shows.

Week 30: Day 2 (page 159)

7:10 a.m.; the clock shows the time Beatrice woke up in the morning; count the number of hours starting from the 12 to the 7; count the number of minutes starting from the 12 to the 2 by counting by fives

Week 30: Day 3 (page 160)

3:40 p.m.

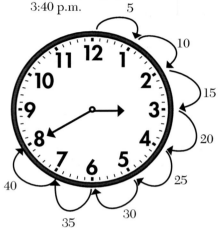

Week 30: Day 4 (page 161)

1. 2:45; Strategy 1: student should have written the time as 2:45 on the digital clock; Strategy 2: student should have drawn the hands on the analog clock to show 2:45 (student may have drawn the hour hand closer to the 3 since the hour will change in 15 more minutes)
2. Possible answer: I like writing the time on a digital clock because I know the number of hours is the first number and the number of minutes is the second number.

Week 30: Day 5 (page 162)

1. The analog clock should show the time as 3:55.
2. The digital clock should show the time as 4:25.
3. Possible answer: I used the analog clock to find the time she finishes her math homework. I started at 3:55 and counted by fives until I counted 30 minutes. Since I passed the number 12, I know the hour changed to 4. She finishes her homework at 4:25 p.m.

Week 31: Day 1 (page 163)

1. Keiko has 2 quarters and 7 pennies.
2. Find the amount of money Keiko has in her piggy bank.
3. Possible answer: I can add 25 and 25 for the two quarters. Then, I can add 7 more for the pennies to find the total amount in her piggy bank.

Week 31: Day 2 (page 164)

57 cents; 25 + 25 = 50; 1 + 1 + 1 + 1 + 1 + 1 = 7; 50 + 7 = 57; Keiko has 2 quarters and 7 pennies; add 25 and 25 for the two quarters; add 7 more for the pennies

#51614—180 Days of Problem Solving

ANSWER KEY *(cont.)*

Week 31: Day 3 (page 165)

Colleen earned 44 cents.

Week 31: Day 4 (page 166)

1. Accept any reasonable answer that shows coins in the amount of 72 cents; Strategy 1: student may have 2 quarters, 2 dimes, and 2 pennies; Strategy 2: student may have 1 quarter, 3 dimes, 3 nickels, and 2 pennies
2. Possible answer: For the first strategy, I used only three types of coins to make 72 cents. For the second strategy, I used four different types of coins to make 72 cents. Both coin collections make 72 cents.

Week 31: Day 5 (page 167)

1. Accept any answer that shows Caitlin has the most money and Mickey has more money than Kimberly. Possible answer:

	Dollar	Quarter	Dime	Nickel	Penny	Total
Caitlin	1	2	3	2	7	$1.97
Mickey	0	3	2	4	2	$1.17
Kimberly	0	1	2	1	3	$0.53

2. Possible story problem: Caitlin has $1.97 to spend at the snack shack. Mickey has $1.17 to spend at the snack shack. Kimberly has $0.53 to spend at the snack shack. How much more money does Caitlin have than Mickey? How much more money does Mickey have than Kimberly?

Week 32: Day 1 (page 168)

1. Mr. Jackson's students measured their bean plants to see how much they grew. They made a line plot to show the length of the bean plants.
2. Possible question: How many bean plants are 3 or more inches?
3. The shortest bean plants are 1 inch. The tallest bean plants are 7 inches. The axis at the bottom of the line plot is labeled with inches.

Week 32: Day 2 (page 169)

4 bean plants; Mr. Jackson's students measured their bean plants; they made a line plot to show the heights of the bean plants; count the number of Xs for 3 on the line plot

Week 32: Day 3 (page 170)

Tomato Plant Growth

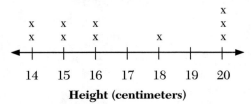

Height (centimeters)

Week 32: Day 4 (page 171)

1. Strategy 1: student should have shown the data in the table; Strategy 2: student should have shown the data using the line plot.

Toy airplane	Length (in inches)
1	9
2	6
3	7
4	5
5	3
6	6
7	2
8	4
9	5
10	7

Toy Airplane Length

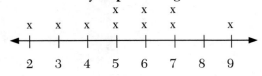

Length (inches)

2. Possible answer: I like showing the data on a line plot better than in a table because I can see the number of bean plants for each height more easily.

ANSWER KEY *(cont.)*

Week 32: Day 5 (page 172)

1. Accept any reasonable measurement for each shoe in the table.
2. Student should have ordered the lengths of the shoes from shortest to longest.
3. Student should have created a line plot to show the lengths of the shoes. Student should have written a title, a label for the axis, numbered the tick marks, and made Xs to show the number of shoes for each length.

Week 33: Day 1 (page 173)

1. The bar graph shows the number of meters four kids ran at school.
2. The heights of the bars show the number of meters each kid ran.
3. Possible questions: Which kid ran the most meters? Which kid ran the fewest meters?

Week 33: Day 2 (page 174)

15 meters; 35 − 20 = 15; bar graph shows the number of meters four kids ran at school; find the number of meters Miguel ran and the number of meters Eduardo ran; subtract to find how many more meters Miguel ran than Eduardo

Week 33: Day 3 (page 175)

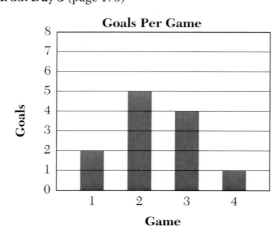

Week 33: Day 4 (page 176)

1. Strategy 1: student should have completed the data in the table; Strategy 2: student should have shown the data in the bar graph

Game	Baskets
1	8
2	5
3	4
4	6

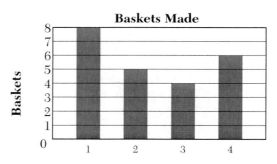

2. Possible answer: I think showing the data on a bar graph is better than a table because I can compare the number of baskets Bree made for each game more easily.

Week 33: Day 5 (page 177)

1.

Girl	Yards
Laura	3
Maria	5
Sarah	2
Jean	5

2. Possible answer:

Title: Football Distance

ANSWER KEY (cont.)

Week 34: Day 1 (page 178)
1. The shape has 3 sides and 3 angles.
2. Name the shape.
3. No; A shape with 3 sides will always create 3 angles. The number of sides and angles will always be the same.

Week 34: Day 2 (page 179)
Triangle; drawing should show a closed figure with 3 sides and 3 angles; shape has 3 sides and 3 angles; draw a picture of a triangle with 3 equal sides and 3 equal angles

Week 34: Day 3 (page 180)
Hexagon; Student should have drawn two circles around the triangles and 3 Xs on the quadrilaterals (rectangle, parallelogram, trapezoid)

Week 34: Day 4 (page 181)
1. Picture 1: student should have drawn a picture using a triangle, quadrilateral, and a pentagon; Picture 2: student should have drawn a picture using a different type of triangle, quadrilateral, and a pentagon; for a quadrilateral, student may have drawn a square, rectangle, rhombus, parallelogram, or trapezoid
2. Possible answer: Both strategies have one triangle, one quadrilateral, and one pentagon. For my first picture, I drew a triangle with 3 equal sides and 3 equal angles, a rectangle, and a pentagon with 5 equal sides and 5 equal angles. For my second picture, I drew a triangle with 3 different sides and 3 different angles, a square, and a pentagon with 5 different sides and angles.

Week 34: Day 5 (page 182)
Student should have drawn a picture of a closed 4-sided figure and a closed 3-sided figure; Possible answer: I drew a rhombus and an equilateral triangle. The rhombus has 4 equal sides and looks like a diamond. An equilateral triangle has 3 equal sides and 3 equal angles.

Week 35: Day 1 (page 183)
1. There is a rectangle.
2. How to partition the rectangle into 8 squares of the same size.
3. Possible answer: I can partition the rectangle into 2 rows with 4 squares in each row.

Week 35: Day 2 (page 184)
Possible answers: 2 rows of 4 squares; 4 rows of 2 squares; 1 row of 8 squares; 8 rows of 1 square; there is a rectangle; partition the rectangle into 8 squares of the same size; student may have drawn a picture to show their answer

Week 35: Day 3 (page 185)
15 equal squares; students should have partitioned the rectangle into 5 rows and 3 columns

Week 35: Day 4 (page 186)
1. Student should have shown two different ways to partition a rectangle into 6 equal squares; Possible strategies: 2 rows and 3 squares in each row; 3 rows and 2 squares in each row; 1 row and 6 squares in each row; 6 rows and 1 square in each row
2. Possible answer: For Rectangle 1, I drew 2 rows with 3 squares in each row. For Rectangle 2, I drew 3 rows with 2 squares in each row. They have a different number of rows and a different number of squares in each row. They both have a total of 6 squares.

Week 35: Day 5 (page 187)
1. 24
2. Possible answers: 6 rows with 4 squares in each row; 2 rows with 12 squares in each row; 12 rows with 2 squares in each row; 3 rows with 8 squares in each row; 8 rows with 3 squares in each row; 1 row with 24 squares in each row; 24 rows with 1 square in each row

Week 36: Day 1 (page 188)
1. There is a circle.
2. Partition the circle into two equal parts.
3. Possible answer: I need to draw a line through the center of the circle to make two equal parts.

ANSWER KEY *(cont.)*

Week 36: Day 2 (page 189)

Halves; student should have drawn a line to partition the circle into halves; student may have drawn a vertical line, horizontal line, or a diagonal line; there is a circle; draw a line through the center of the circle to make two equal parts

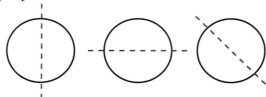

Week 36: Day 3 (page 190)

1. 2 equal parts

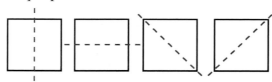

2. 3 equal parts

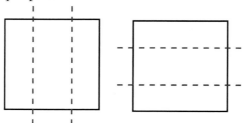

Week 36: Day 4 (page 191)

1. Student should have partitioned the rectangle into fourths two different ways; student may have partitioned the rectangle by drawing vertical lines, horizontal lines, or a combination of the two

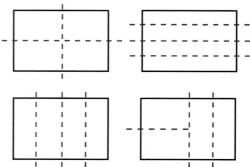

2. Possible answer: I partitioned both rectangles into fourths. They both have 4 equal parts. I partitioned the first rectangle by drawing vertical lines to make 4 equal parts. I partitioned the second rectangle by drawing horizontal lines to make 4 equal parts.

Week 36: Day 5 (page 192)

1. two halves

2. three thirds

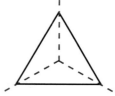

3. four fourths

PRACTICE PAGE RUBRIC

Directions: Evaluate student work in each category by choosing one number in each row. Students have opportunities to score up to four points in each row and up to 16 points total.

	Advanced	Proficient	Developing	Beginning
Problem-solving strategies	Uses multiple efficient strategies Uses a detailed and appropriate visual model	Uses appropriate strategies Uses an appropriate visual model	Demonstrates some form of strategic approach Uses a visual model but is incomplete	No strategic approach is evident No visual model is attempted
Points	4	3	2	1
Mathematical knowledge	Provides correct solutions and multiple solutions when relevant Connects and applies the concept in complex ways	Provides correct solutions Demonstrates proficiency of concept	Shows some correct solutions Demonstrates some proficiency of concept	No solutions are correct Does not demonstrate proficiency of concept
Points	4	3	2	1
Explanation	Explains and justifies thinking thoroughly and clearly	Explains and justifies thinking	Explains thinking but difficult to follow	Offers no explanation of thinking
Points	4	3	2	1
Organization	Well-planned, well-organized, and complete	Shows a plan and is complete	Shows some planning and is mostly complete	Shows no planning and is mostly incomplete
Points	4	3	2	1

PRACTICE PAGE ITEM ANALYSIS

Directions: Record students' rubric scores (page 211) for the Day 5 practice page in the appropriate columns. Add the totals and record the sums in the Total Scores column. You can view: (1) which students are not understanding the mathematical concepts and problem-solving steps, and (2) how students progress after multiple encounters with the problem-solving process.

Student Name	Week 1	Week 2	Week 3	Week 4	Week 5	Week 6	Week 7	Week 8	Week 9	Total Scores
Average Class Score										

PRACTICE PAGE ITEM ANALYSIS *(cont.)*

Directions: Record students' rubric scores (page 211) for the Day 5 practice page in the appropriate columns. Add the totals and record the sums in the Total Scores column. You can view: (1) which students are not understanding the mathematical concepts and problem-solving steps, and (2) how students progress after multiple encounters with the problem-solving process.

Student Name	Week 10	Week 11	Week 12	Week 13	Week 14	Week 15	Week 16	Week 17	Week 18	Total Scores
Average Class Score										

PRACTICE PAGE ITEM ANALYSIS *(cont.)*

Directions: Record students' rubric scores (page 211) for the Day 5 practice page in the appropriate columns. Add the totals and record the sums in the Total Scores column. You can view: (1) which students are not understanding the mathematical concepts and problem-solving steps, and (2) how students progress after multiple encounters with the problem-solving process.

Student Name	Week 19	Week 20	Week 21	Week 22	Week 23	Week 24	Week 25	Week 26	Week 27	Total Scores
Average Class Score										

PRACTICE PAGE ITEM ANALYSIS *(cont.)*

Directions: Record students' rubric scores (page 211) for the Day 5 practice page in the appropriate columns. Add the totals and record the sums in the Total Scores column. You can view: (1) which students are not understanding the mathematical concepts and problem-solving steps, and (2) how students progress after multiple encounters with the problem-solving process.

Student Name	Week 28	Week 29	Week 30	Week 31	Week 32	Week 33	Week 34	Week 35	Week 36	Total Scores
Average Class Score										

STUDENT ITEM ANALYSIS

Directions: Record individual student's rubric scores (page 211) for each practice page in the appropriate columns. Add the totals and record the sums in the Total Scores column. You can view: (1) which concepts and problem-solving steps the student is not understanding and (2) how the student is progressing after multiple encounters with the problem-solving process.

Student Name:	Day 1	Day 2	Day 3	Day 4	Day 5	Total Scores
Week 1						
Week 2						
Week 3						
Week 4						
Week 5						
Week 6						
Week 7						
Week 8						
Week 9						
Week 10						
Week 11						
Week 12						
Week 13						
Week 14						
Week 15						
Week 16						
Week 17						
Week 18						
Week 19						
Week 20						
Week 21						
Week 22						
Week 23						
Week 24						
Week 25						
Week 26						
Week 27						
Week 28						
Week 29						
Week 30						
Week 31						
Week 32						
Week 33						
Week 34						
Week 35						
Week 36						

#51614—180 Days of Problem Solving © Shell Education

PROBLEM-SOLVING FRAMEWORK

Use the following problem-solving steps to help you:

1. understand the problem
2. make a plan
3. solve the problem
4. check your answer and explain your thinking

What Do You Know?

- read the problem
- say the problem in your own words
- picture the problem
- find the important information
- understand the question

What Is Your Plan?

- draw a picture or model
- choose a strategy
- choose an operation (+, −)
- decide how many steps there are

Solve the Problem!

- carry out your plan
- check your steps
- decide if your strategy works or choose a new strategy
- find the answer

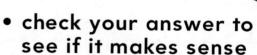

Look Back and Explain!

- check your answer to see if it makes sense
- decide if there are other possible answers
- use words to explain your answer

PROBLEM-SOLVING STRATEGIES

Draw a picture.	Make a table or list.	Use a number sentence.
		$10 + 4 = 14$

Make a model.	Look for a pattern.	Act it out.
Whole 19 — **Part** 10 — **Part** 9	 3, 6, 9, 12, 15, __18__	

Solve a simpler problem.	Work backward.	Use logical reasoning.
$7 + 6$ $7 + 3 + 3$ $10 + 3 = 13$	⟵ ☐ $+ 3 + 5 = 18$	

Guess and check.	Create a graph.	Use concrete objects.
$2 + ☐ + 5 = 11$ $2 + 4 + 5 = 11$ $11 = 11$ Yes!	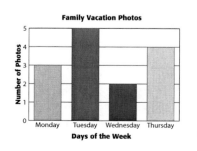	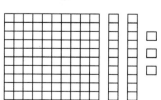 base-ten blocks

DIGITAL RESOURCES

Teacher Resources

Resource	Filename
Practice Page Rubric	rubric.pdf
Practice Page Item Analysis	itemanalysis.pdf itemanalysis.docx itemanalysis.xlsx
Student Item Analysis	studentitem.pdf studentitem.docx studentitem.xlsx

Student Resources

Resource	Filename
Problem-Solving Framework	framework.pdf
Problem-Solving Strategies	strategies.pdf

NOTES

NOTES

NOTES

NOTES

NOTES